Coping with
Crisis Situations
in the Classroom

Coping with Crisis Situations in the Classroom

Stuart E. Schwartz

PRENTICE HALL, Englewood Cliffs, New Jersey 07632

P. T
Sch 96
1990

Library of Congress Cataloging-in-Publication Data

Schwartz, Stuart E.
   Coping with crisis situations in the classroom / Stuart E.
Schwartz.
       p.   cm.
   Originally published: Dealing with the unexpected. Belmont, Calif.
: Wadsworth, 1983.
   Bibliography: p.
   ISBN 0-13-382334-2
   1. Classroom management--Study and teaching--Simulation methods.
2. Crisis management--Study and teaching--Simulation methods.
I. Schwartz, Stuart E. Dealing with the unexpected. II. Title.
LB3013.S39 1990
371.1'02--dc20   89-35706
                                                                CIP

Editorial/production supervision: Nancy Menges
Cover design: Jeannette Jacobs
Manufacturing buyer: Robert Anderson

 © 1990 by Prentice-Hall, Inc.
A Division of Simon & Schuster
Englewood Cliffs, New Jersey 07632

Previously published by Wadsworth under the title
Dealing with the Unexpected.

Printed in the United States of America

10 9 8 7 6 5 4 3 2 1

ISBN   0-13-382334-2

Prentice-Hall International (UK) Limited, *London*
Prentice-Hall of Australia Pty. Limited, *Sydney*
Prentice-Hall Canada Inc., *Toronto*
Prentice-Hall Hispanoamericana, S.A., *Mexico*
Prentice-Hall of India Private Limited, *New Delhi*
Prentice-Hall of Japan, Inc., *Tokyo*
Prentice-Hall of Southeast Asia Pte. Ltd., *Singapore*
Editora Prentice-Hall do Brasil, Ltda., *Rio de Janeiro*

To my parents —
for their strength,
love, and teaching.

Contents

Preface

I will never forget my first day of student teaching. I met my directing teacher and promptly was given a back seat so that I could observe. Watching her interacting with about thirty elementary school children was fascinating. She would praise, scold, smile, frown, act, react, anticipate, and control the entire group with ease and grace. I quickly realized that she was doing much more than teaching subject matter.

As I assumed the role of student teacher in that classroom and the role of teacher in subsequent assignments at the junior and senior high levels, I repeatedly observed the same situation. I realized that teachers don't just teach.

Even as a professor of education it is easy for me to observe that presenting a good lecture is not my only responsibility. As is true with any teacher, I must be ready to comfort or aid one of my college students who is distressed or ill. I must deal with unexpected student comments, parents' phone calls, other professors' statements, and administrative decisions. As a professor I am also seen as the person who should be able to make split-second decisions if an emergency, such as a building fire or a student injury, should occur.

But in all of my own training had I been prepared to deal with the myriad of unexpected events that could face teachers? Even though I had completed three teacher training programs, the answer was clearly no.

Because of my concern for this lack of preparation to deal with the unexpected, I began a few years ago to conduct simulation exercises in my teacher training courses at the University of Florida. I also began including simulations of unexpected events during in-service workshops. The reactions of the participating college students and teachers and the demand for workshops on this topic have clearly shown me that the use of simulations and preparation for dealing with crises is definitely welcomed and desired by educators. Teachers want to think about and prepare themselves for those unexpected events that they know will happen.

This book was developed to help meet the need for training teachers to handle the unexpected. The content and procedures have been evaluated during the book's formative stage. Selected chapters were field tested at the summative stage by undergraduate and graduate students in education. The feedback received has strongly been supportive of the book's content, exercises, and activities.

I urge all teacher training programs to include preparation for the unexpected in their curricula. The content of this book and additional advice and suggestions given by instructors, inservice trainers, and professors should be extremely valuable. Every teacher trained in dealing with unexpected events should be much better prepared for all of the responsibilities of education.

This book was developed to assist preservice and inservice teachers in dealing with unexpected events. It is appropriate for persons who teach any subject and for educators at all levels—from preschool through college. Completion of the exercises in this book will help you, the teacher, prepare for the handling of difficult, unexpected situations as they arise. Role-playing the simulations during courses or inservice workshops will give you an opportunity to observe actual problems and then rehearse possible solutions.

The book is organized into nine chapters. The first chapter gives you a rationale for the contents and directions for using the book. Here you will learn the importance of simulation activities in teacher training. You will be given directions on how to complete the exercises, and a sample exercise with response guidelines will be presented.

Chapters 2 through 8 will present you with samples of unexpected problems that teachers have faced in the past. You will be given many suggestions for handling the problems. Then you will be asked to complete the pre-simulation exercises as preparation for in-class or workshop role-play activities. Once the exercises are completed, your group will act out the problems and discuss their solutions.

In Chapter 2 you will be presented with a variety of behavior problems exhibited by students. Chapter 3 reviews difficulties regarding the health and safety of your students. The personal problems of students will be addressed in Chapter 4.

After attending to those unexpected events teachers face with students, you will have an opportunity to consider your interactions with others. Chapter 5 will present you with difficulties that may arise in dealing with parents. In Chapter 6 you will address unexpected events involving other school staff members.

Ways in which a teacher's personal life may be affected by unexpected events is the next topic. This discussion will be found in Chapter 7.

A section of the book designed specifically for preservice teachers will follow. In Chapter 8 you will have a chance to review unexpected problems that are related to the role of student teacher.

The final section, Chapter 9, will give you many hints and suggestions that will be helpful as you handle unexpected events. Here you will also find special ideas for dealing with emergencies, handicapped pupils, and particular age groups.

All of the events described in this book have actually occurred. The names of the participants, however, have been changed.

Acknowledgments

I wish to specifically acknowledge four individuals for their help in preparing this book. My sincere thanks go to my colleagues Bob Algozzine, Bill Powell, and Richard Voorneveld for their critical reading of the manuscript and for their many suggestions. I also want to express my appreciation to Leila Cantara for her excellent organizing, editing, and typing.

Thanks also go to the following individuals for their work and suggestions as manuscript reviewers:

Professor John Umbreit
Special Education Department
University of Arizona
Tucson, AZ 85721

Professor Richard D. Shepardson
Division of Early Childhood & Elementary
   Education
University of Iowa
N259 Lindquist Center
Iowa City, IA 52242

Professor Joan C. Carson
Curriculum and Instruction Department
University of Mississippi
University, MS 38677

Professor Douglas J. Stanwyck
Educational Foundations Department
Georgia State University
Atlanta, GA 30303

Professor Harold L. Wilson
Psychology and Counselor Education
Central Missouri State University
Warrensburg, MO 64093

Professor George Rawlins
Education Department
Austin Peay State University
Clarksville, TN 37040

Professor Meryl E. Englander
Educational Psychology Department
Indiana University
Bloomington, IN 47401

—Stuart E. Schwartz

Chapter 1

Introduction

I vividly recall the first day of my teaching career. After a complete college-level teacher-training program I was about to face my own students. What was I going to do? How would I organize myself? What would I teach? I frantically searched my college class notes, thought about all of my practicum and student teaching experiences, and prepared myself for that first teaching day when I would finally be responsible for my own pupils.

I knew I was able to assess student performance. I knew I was able to plan an appropriate curriculum. I knew about individual differences among students. I was able to evaluate and select instructional materials. I had some idea of how to group my students and use various teaching techniques. In many ways I was quite well prepared and competent.

This book is not about all of those things teachers typically do and are generally prepared to do. It is a book designed to help you ready yourself for events that happen to every educator but are usually not even discussed in the teacher-training curriculum.

What are these events? They are the unexpected interruptions, emergencies, disruptions, intrusions, and other extraordinary events that we teachers pray will never happen to us. But *they do occur*, and this book is designed to acquaint you with a variety of possible events and give you an opportunity to prepare for them before they actually happen to you.

The events presented here have occurred in elementary and secondary and in regular and special education settings. It would be wise for you to consider if your reactions would be different for various age ranges or ability groups. If your class or seminar is specializing in one age range or type of child, try to consider that during your preparation for and conduction of the simulations.

Simulations can be an extremely valuable part of your education. Merely reading about these events is not enough preparation; actually rehearsing the handling of unexpected events will give you realistic experiences—experiences that you can utilize when teaching. The simulations offer you an opportunity to think about your reactions, attitudes, beliefs, style, and ability regarding the handling of unexpected situations. The simulations also offer you the chance to use your ideas, manipulate and modify them, and reject or accept them in a safe environment.

In this book, you have an opportunity to prepare yourself for the simulations by completing pre-simulation exercises. These are the questions that follow each simulation under *Reactions*, *Effects*, and *Notes*. Just as in real-life situations, it is impossible to predict exactly what will occur in the simulations and how you and the other people involved in a given situation will react. Thus it is difficult for you to be precise in stating what you would do. Being as thorough as possible and planning for a variety of conditions in the pre-simulation exercises, however, will definitely assist you.

After you have read the simulations and completed the pre-simulation exercises, the simulations will be acted out in your college classroom or teacher-training workshop. One person from your group will play the role of teacher. Others will be asked to assume roles necessary for the particular event. Then the simulation will be conducted with the participants acting out the situation. The participants should act the way they believe that persons in real-life situations would act.

After the simulation, all of the persons involved should discuss and critique the way the person who had the teacher's role handled the event. Explore all possible solutions or reactions to each problem. Then discuss the consequences of the teacher's behaviors or reactions and the consequences of the reactions suggested by members of the group.

It is important to keep in mind that in almost every case there are a number of ways to have reacted. Don't be concerned about a right or wrong way—be concerned that the person who played the role of teacher reacted in a responsible, reasonable, efficient, and professional manner, and that the outcome appeared to be positive.

If you are the one in the role of teacher, try to stay calm as you go through the exercise. Quickly consider your alternatives before you react. Try to think of the consequences of your reaction in terms of your school and principal, the students involved, the students' parents, and yourself.

Try not to concern yourself with what your peers are thinking—remember, you are the teacher in charge and it is much easier to react from the sidelines than from the front of the room. Remember that after your simulation you may need to defend what you did. Be able to admit your mistakes and learn from these experiences. It is much better to go through these simulations in the safety of your college classroom or inservice workshop and err than to handle one of these events in a real classroom incorrectly.

When you are observing and reacting to another person's simulation, remember: Your turn will come, whether in your class, a workshop, or out in the real world. As you see the event unfold, attempt to consider quickly all possible ways in which you would have reacted if you were the teacher. Think of the consequences of the teacher's behavior. Determine if the person playing the teacher's role reacted the same way you would have. If the reactions were different, which way was better? Observe, think, and try to realize what you really would have or should have done if you were confronted with this particular event in your own classroom.

Many teachers and teacher trainees never stop to think about all of the unexpected events that could happen to them. The completion of the sampling of events in this reaction book should help you be well prepared for the real world of unpredictable occurrences in your classroom. Know how to develop curriculum, know how to assess, know how to teach, know how to do all of the things that are usually part of the teacher-training curriculum. But above all, know how to handle the unexpected in your classroom. This reaction book was designed to help prepare you for these events.

Have fun—and stay calm.

Directions for the Pre-simulation Exercises (Reactions, Effects, and Notes)

Your first step should be to read through the simulations in this book. Try to imagine yourself as the teacher in a role-playing situation or as the teacher in real life. Consider all of the ways you could or should react to each event. Then think about the consequences of your actions.

As you read the simulations, record all of your responses to the questions in the spaces provided. You will be asked questions regarding what you would say or do. You will be asked to state the reasons for your actions and responses. Then you will be expected to reflect upon the effects of your own behaviors.

The first section following the description of the simulation is entitled *Reactions*. Here you will have questions that ask about your objectives. Tell what you hope to accomplish through your words and actions. Discuss immediate and long-term objectives.

You will also be asked to state what you will say and do. Be as precise as possible in explaining what you think you would say or do in the situation.

In some simulations you will be asked if you will involve others. State who they are and why you will contact them, and make notes regarding what you will say.

For some of the simulations, you will be requested to suggest how you can avoid circumstances like those presented. These questions should help you focus on your ability to curtail the occurrence of difficult situations.

Once you have responded to the questions regarding your reactions, you will have an opportunity to address the ramifications of your actions and responses. In this section, called *Effects*, you should discuss how your behaviors will influence, control, change, or in any way affect the other persons involved. There will always be a chance for you to reflect upon the effects of your behaviors on the principal and/or school. This question should help you consider how your principal will feel about the way you handled a particular problem. It will also allow you to think about how your actions will reflect upon the entire school community.

The final question regarding effects of your actions and responses pertains to you. Here is where you should ponder the effects of the event and your behaviors on you as a person and teacher. Consider your health, safety, professional status, legal obligations, and emotional status as you respond to this question.

Following the reactions and effects will be a *Notes* section. Special reminders on resources, what not to do, and alternative reactions may be appropriate here. The special notes you take immediately following simulations will prove helpful for future reference.

Answering the questions in the exercises will help you prepare to react to these events as you and your peers role-play the simulations. Your responses will also assist you if you are selected to portray the teacher. Most importantly, your preparation will help you if these or similar events occur when you are in a real classroom— where you have responsibility for student growth, health, education, safety, and emotional development.

A Sample Exercise

This sample simulation is presented to aid you in responding to the exercises in this book. First read the simulation description. Then read the questions and write your responses in the provided spaces. Try to answer all of the questions thoroughly.

When you are finished, review the guidelines given immediately after the space for notes. Check to see if you have been thorough in your responses. Be sure that you have considered alternate ways to have handled the event. Then review your responses to the questions regarding effects of your actions. Be sure that you have given careful thought to the consequences of your behaviors.

Once you have reviewed the guidelines and your responses to the questions, you should be ready to complete the rest of the pre-simulation exercises in the book. Remember that all of the simulations are based upon real experiences and that they can happen again. Your efforts today will help you be prepared for the realities of tomorrow.

Sample Simulation

Setting:	Your classroom
Time:	While showing a movie to your class
Persons involved:	Sara (one of your students) and the rest of your pupils
Background information:	Sara has often misbehaved in your classroom. On many occasions she has fallen, tipped over her chair, and dropped books.
Circumstances:	While the movie is being shown, Sara begins to tilt back in her chair. You tell her to stop so that she won't fall.
Simulation:	A few minutes later, Sara tilts her chair again and falls with a crash. All the students laugh and snicker. You scold Sara and tell her to get up and to behave herself. She picks herself up slowly and appears to be in pain. She then sits down and begins to cry.

Reactions

1. What are your objectives? _____

_____

_____

_____

2. What will you do? _____

_____

_____

_____

3. If you determine that Sara is injured, what will you do? Say?

_____

_____

_____

4. If you determine that Sara is not injured, what will you do?

Say? _____

_____

_____

_____

_____

Effects   What effects will your actions and responses have upon Sara?

_____

_____

_____

The other students?   _____

_____

_____

_____

Your principal/school?   _____

_____

_____

_____

You?   _____

_____

_____

Notes   _____

_____

_____

_____

_____

_____

_____

_____

_____

_____

Guidelines

Reactions

1. Have you considered
   a. if Sara were injured?
   b. Sara's history of disruptive behavior?
   c. that your movie/lesson was interrupted?
   d. the behavior of the other students?
2. Will you
   a. determine if Sara is injured?
   b. stop the movie? turn on the lights?
   c. ignore Sara's behavior and crying?
   d. scold the other students?
   e. remove Sara from class?
   f. punish Sara?
3. Should you
   a. send Sara to the office?
   b. send Sara to the school nurse?
   c. call the office or nurse?
   d. tell Sara that you're concerned about her injury?
   e. give appropriate first aid?
   f. follow school procedures for accidents/injuries?
4. Will you
   a. scold Sara privately?
   b. scold Sara publicly?
   c. ignore Sara's behavior?
   d. continue the movie?
   e. send Sara to the office?
   f. punish Sara?
   g. call Sara's parents?

Effects

Sara. Will your behaviors reduce any additional injury? Increase or decrease the possibility of this behavior occurring again?

The other students. Will your behaviors demonstrate to the other students that you are in control? That you are concerned about everyone's safety? That your lesson is important?

Your principal/school. Will your behaviors make the principal upset regarding school procedures for injuries? Make the school liable for negligence?

You. Will you question whether you have taken the right action? Will you be satisfied with your knowledge of first aid? Will you feel as though you have gained or lost respect or control?

As you work through the simulations in the book, realize that a thorough job now should help you plan for unexpected events in your classroom. Consider all alternatives, the consequences of your actions, and how your actions will affect the school, family, and students. Think about yourself as well. Be sure you safeguard yourself physically, emotionally, and legally.

Once you complete the pre-simulation exercises, you and your class or workshop group will be ready to conduct the simulations. That will be your opportunity to try your ideas, experiment with approaches to problems, and rehearse different methods of handling unexpected events. You will also have a chance to discuss the experiences with your instructor, workshop leader, and peers. All of these activities are designed with you in mind as you enter a classroom where you have full responsibility.

Directions for the Simulations

Simulations should be conducted by the *simulation director*—the course professor, the inservice leader, or a member of the group. It is the responsibility of the simulation director to conduct the following eight steps. Since it is impossible to predict how each simulation will evolve, some direction and advice may be needed during the actual simulations.

   1. Select one member of the group or

class to play the teacher's role. Have that person leave the room or area.

2. Select one simulation from a particular chapter or from the entire book. Choose persons to assume the various roles as indicated in the *persons involved* section of the simulation. Make any necessary arrangements to the area or "stage" being used for the simulation. This would include such things as setting up several student desks or a teacher's desk.

3. Have the "teacher" return to the room or area. Explain the setting and background information to that person. The time (if pertinent), persons involved, and circumstances should be explained. All participants should then act out the described event. The "teacher" should handle the event as if it were real.

Note: In some simulations it is impossible to completely act out the desired reaction. For instance, if the "teacher" observed a car theft it would be appropriate to telephone the police. During the simulation the "teacher" should only state, "Now I would call the police and say. . ."

4. Indicate that the event is completed after the "teacher" has had a sufficient opportunity to react to the unexpected event. Most simulations should take from three to ten minutes to conduct.

5. Give the "teacher" an opportunity to explain what else would need to be done toward the resolution of the problems presented.

6. Conduct a group discussion that addresses the performance of the "teacher." Remember that most often there are many ways for the events to have been handled.

7. Allow the "teacher" to offer reasons for the manner in which the simulation was handled, for the statements made, and for the action taken.

8. Conclude the discussion with consideration of the consequences of the "teacher's" reactions upon others who may be directly or indirectly involved. Consider major do's and don't's. Try to reach consensus regarding the best ways to react to this particular event or similar events, should they occur in real-life situations.

Simulation Director's Checklist

_____ 1. Select and excuse teacher.

_____ 2. Choose simulation. Arrange stage area.

_____ 3. Bring teacher into room. Explain setting and situation. Conduct simulation.

_____ 4. End simulation.

_____ 5. Ask teacher to explain future actions.

_____ 6. Conduct discussion regarding teacher's performance.

_____ 7. Request teacher to explain his or her reactions.

_____ 8. Discuss consequences of teacher's reactions and "best" ways to handle this event.

Remember: All of the simulations in this book are real. These events have happened and they can happen again.

Chapter 2

Behavior Problems

Almost all teachers have received some training in behavior control. Different approaches, such as behavior management, contingency management, punishment, counseling, isolation, and suspension, may be selected and utilized. These methods, when used reasonably and consistently, will often have the desired result of keeping behavior in control so learning can occur.

You probably feel confident in your behavior control skills, but are you ready for those unexpected behavioral disruptions that need your immediate and complete attention? For those events that defy the use of your adopted management system? For those crises that may, in fact, be dangerous for you and your students? Well, the purpose of this chapter is to help prepare you for those serious behavior problems—the events we have heard about and wished would never happen to us.

Factors to Consider

Picture yourself walking down the street. A stranger walks over to you, flashes a knife, and demands your money. What would you do? Your action would probably depend upon your own self-defense ability and upon your estimate of the intent and skills of the robber.

You would be at a disadvantage for a number of reasons: You would be surprised or shocked by the event and perhaps overcome by fear. You would have no knowledge of the robber's history. And, you would not be seen as an authority figure.

Now consider a behavior problem with a student and the factors mentioned above. As a teacher you would have a good knowledge of your ability to handle the situation. You should have some knowledge of the student's intent, history, and skills. Although the specific event would be a surprise, you should be able to maintain enough composure so that you could act deliberately and not out of fear. Further, you would be seen as an authority figure by the student.

This comparison should suggest to you that as a teacher you usually have four distinct advantages in dealing with unexpected behavioral problems. Let's consider them.

1. *You know how to react and know your ability to act during an event involving a student's misbehavior.* You know what resources, such as other teachers, the principal, and school guards (employed by a growing number of schools), are available. And you would know what school district procedures are expected to be followed during a serious behavior event.

2. *You know the student who is involved.* From prior school experiences you may be able to predict the student's next move. You also would know if the student is following an established pattern.

3. *You are able to remain calm.* If you approach the problem in a deliberate manner and demonstrate that you are not upset, then others involved would expect that you are able to control the outcome of events.

4. *You are an authority figure.* As a teacher you would have some level of respect from the students, or at least the students would know that you are recognized as in charge by the school administration.

In addition to the four advantages there are twelve suggestions you should consider as you deal with these events.

1. *Don't give trouble a chance to start.* Keep your students interested and involved. That way they won't have time to get into trouble.

2. *When trouble arises, listen to those involved.* Perhaps the problem is totally a misunderstanding. With your ability to listen and objectively understand the problem, you may be able to end the difficulty quickly.

3. *If the problem involves a conflict between two students, help them stop.* Students are often motivated by peer pressure to continue an argument or fight. Your direction to stop may be all that is needed.

4. *Be seen and heard as the boss.* Don't cower in a corner and whisper a command. Step up front and shout the orders if needed.

5. *Remember the facts.* Know what prompted the problem. Perhaps similar conditions can be avoided in the future. Also, know the details—who, what, when, where, why, and how—so that you can make a report to your principal later.

6. *Don't assume guilt.* It is quite dangerous to take one student's word over another's. It is likewise unwise to think that someone has done wrong. Know the facts before you act.

7. *Don't make a big deal out of a little issue.* By treating a difficult problem quietly and with restraint, it may seem to others to have been minor in nature.

8. *Be fair.* Treat all of your students alike. Then, when a problem does arise, you won't be accused of favoring a particular student.

9. *When you punish, do so soon after the problem and be sure the student understands why he or she is being punished.* Also give choices of punishment, whenever possible, to avoid a "this or else" conflict.

10. *Accentuate the positive.* Try to give attention to good behavior. Many times bad behavior is exhibited to gain attention. If good behavior consistently gets more attention, perhaps students will choose that avenue.

11. *Don't give up control.* Establish that you are the boss on your first day and keep it that way. You can always loosen your grip later, but it is usually difficult to regain it.

12. *Get help when you need it.* Don't try to be a hero and independently handle a life-threatening problem. Call for aid. Know your school's procedure for summoning assistance.

By keeping these advantages and guidelines in mind, you should be better prepared to handle any challenge. Most of your students, their parents, and your principal will think very highly of you if you can create a learning environment that is safe and comfortable. When you've handled a serious behavior problem well, you can likewise feel good about being in control of your classroom.

Think About It

Here's your opportunity to do some serious brainstorming. In the left-hand column below, briefly describe eight behavior problems you have seen or anticipate seeing in classrooms. Then, below each, state two possible solutions to the problems.

1. _____

   a. _____

     _____

   b. _____

     _____

2. _____

   a. _____

     _____

   b. _____

3. _____

   a. _____

     _____

   b. _____

4. _____

   a. _____

     _____

   b. _____

     _____

5. _____

   a. _____

     _____

   b. _____

     _____

6. _____

   a. _____

     _____

   b. _____

     _____

7. _____

   a. _____

     _____

   b. _____

     _____

8. _____

   a. _____

     _____

   b. _____

     _____

Simulations

Some of the simulations on the following pages are rather mild. Others may prove to be quite severe. In either event you need to prepare yourself to handle events like these since they have occurred—and will continue to occur—in both elementary and secondary classrooms.

Simulation 2.1 **Get Out the Gloves!**

Setting: Your classroom

Time: Between classes

Persons involved: Audrey Swanson, Cindy Byerly, and a few of your other students

Background information: A number of your students have reputations for being tough. Audrey and Cindy are in that group.

Circumstances: Audrey and Cindy have been standing in the back of your classroom talking. A few other students have arrived for class. You are standing in the doorway talking to one of the school custodians.

Simulation: All of a sudden you hear screaming and cursing from the back of your room. As you turn you see Cindy falling to the floor and Audrey grabbing a folding chair and raising it over her head.

Reactions

1. What will you do immediately? Why? _____

_____

_____

_____

2. Will you involve the custodian? Why? _____

_____

_____

_____

3. What other actions will you take? _____

_____

_____

_____

4. After you've stopped the fight, what will you do? Say?

_____

_____

_____

_____

_____

5. Is this a matter that should be reported to your principal? To the girls' parents? Why? _____

_____

_____

Effects   What effects will your actions and responses have upon Audrey and Cindy? _____

_____

_____

_____

Your other students? _____

_____

_____

_____

The custodian? _____

_____

_____

_____

Your principal/school? _____

_____

_____

_____

You? _____

_____

_____

_____

Notes   _____

_____

_____

_____

_____

_____

Simulation 2.2 **For Adults Only**

Setting:	Your classroom
Time:	During class
Persons involved:	Sidney, Carl, and Tim (your students)
Background information:	You have had no problems from the three students in the past.
Circumstances:	Your students are working in small groups in different parts of the room.
Simulation:	You notice that Sidney, Carl, and Tim are not attending to their work. As you walk toward the students, Sidney quickly puts a magazine under his books. You ask to see what he has hidden and he hands you a rather risqué magazine. You say, "OK, who brought this little item into class?" They all deny bringing it in.

Reactions

1. What are your possible actions? _____

_____

_____

_____

2. Which one will you choose? Why? _____

_____

_____

_____

3. Should you confiscate the magazine? Why? _____

_____

_____

_____

4. If you find out who brought the magazine into class, what will

you do? _____

_____

_____

_____

5. Is this a matter that should be reported to your principal? To the boys' parents? Why? _____

_____

_____

_____

Effects   What effects will your actions and responses have upon Sidney, Carl, and Tim? _____

_____

_____

_____

Your principal/school? _____

_____

_____

_____

You? _____

_____

_____

_____

Notes   _____

_____

_____

_____

_____

_____

_____

_____

_____

_____

Simulation 2.3 **And the Wall Came Tumblin' Down**

Setting: A hallway in your school—near the student restrooms

Time: Lunch hour

Persons involved: Four students from the school

Background information: Your school has been plagued by acts of vandalism lately. Last week your principal asked all faculty members to keep an extra sharp eye out for vandals. Three teachers per day have been assigned just to walk the halls during lunch period. Today is your day to walk.

Circumstances: You're walking alone down a hallway at the far end of your building. No one else is nearby and all is quiet. Suddenly you hear a loud crash coming from one of the student restrooms and some muffled cheering.

Simulation: You cautiously open the restroom door. Inside you find four very guilty looking students who appear to be shocked by your intrusion. One of the stall walls has been pulled from the restroom wall and is lying on the floor. You say, "OK, let me have your names." The four say, "No way!" So you say, "OK, come with me then." Again they refuse.

Reactions

1. What are your options? _____

_____

_____

2. Which option will you try? Why? _____

_____

_____

_____

3. What will you say to the four students? _____

_____

_____

4. If the students were to physically threaten you, what would you do? _____

_____

_____

5. What could you or your principal have done differently in approaching the vandalism problem? _____

_____

_____

_____

Effects   What effects will your activities and responses have upon the four students? _____

_____

_____

_____

Your principal/school? _____

_____

_____

_____

You? _____

_____

_____

Notes   _____

_____

_____

_____

_____

_____

_____

_____

_____

_____

Simulation 2.4 Do You Blame Her?

Setting:	Your classroom
Time:	During a class period
Persons involved:	Your students and Mr. Parker's students
Background information:	Mr. Parker's class is in your room, along with your students, for this class period. You both arranged for a guest speaker for this lesson. Mr. Parker went to a meeting at the district office, so you are in charge of both groups.
Circumstances:	Your guest speaker is making a somewhat dry presentation to the students. Most of the students, however, are listening respectfully. Twice in the past five minutes the speaker has asked for quiet from a small group of Mr. Parker's students. You finally interrupted and scolded the same small group. The speaker continued her presentation.
Simulation:	All of a sudden the speaker says to the class, "I'm sorry, but your manners are disgusting. I won't speak to a group like this." And she turns to you and says, "I'm sorry, but I'm leaving!" She walks out the door. The room is silent and all eyes are on you.

Reactions

1. What will you say to the entire group? _____

_____

_____

_____

2. What will you say to the small group that seemed to cause the

disturbance? _____

_____

_____

_____

3. Will there be any punishment? Of whom? What would you

consider? _____

_____

_____

_____

4. What will you say to Mr. Parker? _____

_____

_____

5. Will you report this to your principal? Why? _____

_____

_____

Effects What effects will your actions and responses have upon the students? _____

_____

_____

The speaker? _____

_____

_____

Mr. Parker? _____

_____

_____

Your principal/school? _____

_____

_____

You? _____

_____

_____

Notes _____

_____

_____

_____

_____

_____

_____

_____

Simulation 2.5 **Smokers Beware!**

Setting: Your classroom

Time: During a class

Persons involved: Sheldon Brown (one of your students) and the rest of your class

Background information: Sheldon is a constant problem. He has been in trouble in school many times and is doing very poorly in his schoolwork.

Circumstances: Cigarettes are not allowed in your school. Your principal has asked that teachers confiscate any that are found. You are walking across your room to check on a student's work. You glance toward Sheldon and notice that he has a pack of cigarettes in his pocket.

Simulation: You walk over to Sheldon and say, "What's in your pocket?" His response is "nothing." You then say, "Let me have them or you're going to the office." Sheldon won't give you the cigarettes, so you say, "Go to the office right now." He won't do that either. Meanwhile, all work in the room has stopped and everyone is watching the conflict.

Reactions

1. What are you going to do? Say? _____

_____

_____

_____

2. How will you get the class back on its task? _____

_____

_____

_____

3. How could you have avoided this conflict? _____

_____

_____

4. What would happen if you allow Sheldon to keep the cigarettes and stay in the room? _____

_____

_____

Effects What effects will your actions and responses have upon Sheldon? _____

_____

_____

_____

Your other students? _____

_____

_____

_____

Your principal/school? _____

_____

_____

_____

You? _____

_____

_____

_____

Notes _____

_____

_____

_____

_____

_____

_____

_____

_____

_____

Simulation 2.6 **A Violent Reaction**

Setting: Your classroom

Time: Near the end of a class period

Persons involved: Carlos Avellaneda (one of your students) and the rest of your class

Background information: Carlos has been a severe behavior problem. He has been suspended from school before for hitting other students, kicking a teacher, and smashing windows. He is a big fellow, and most students and quite a few teachers are afraid of him.

Circumstances: You've only had a few minor problems with Carlos. Today, however, he seems quite irritated. You have been ignoring him and have not even pushed him to do any work.

Simulation: You are handing back tests that your class did yesterday. Carlos got a score of 38. One of the students asks you what the highest test score was and you say, "The highest was 96 and the lowest was 38." Carlos says softly, but loudly enough so everyone can hear, "Why you #X@##+*$¢%#%!" You look at Carlos and say, "Don't you ever say that again." He jumps out of his seat with teeth clenched and fists raised and starts walking toward you.

Reactions 1. What are your objectives? _____

_____

_____

_____

2. What are your options? _____

_____

_____

3. Which option will you choose? Why? _____

_____

_____

_____

4. If you need help, how will you get it? _____

_____

_____

5. How could you have avoided this conflict? _____

_____

_____

_____

Effects What effects will your actions and responses have upon Carlos?

_____

_____

_____

Your other students? _____

_____

_____

_____

Your principal/school? _____

_____

_____

_____

You? _____

_____

_____

_____

Notes _____

_____

_____

_____

_____

_____

_____

_____

_____

_____

Simulation 2.7 **But How Will He Get Home?**

Setting: Outside, near the loading area for the school buses

Time: In the afternoon, five minutes before the buses leave

Persons involved: Manny Smith, Tim Edgerton, and Thang Nguyen (students from your school)

Background information: You don't know the three students who are involved.

Circumstances: You are on bus duty today and are responsible for all of the students until the buses leave. You are talking to a few pupils when you hear some yelling and screaming from one of the buses.

Simulation: You step onto the bus and say, "What's going on in here?" Manny yells (while pointing at Tim and Thang), "They were hitting me—they always do." With that Manny runs past you and off the bus. You tell Tim and Thang to please behave themselves. Then you get off the bus to talk to Manny. He refuses to get back on the bus. The driver arrives, starts the motor, and yells out the door, "Are you going?" Manny says, "No!"

Reactions 1. What are your options? _____

_____

_____

2. What can you say to Manny? _____

_____

_____

_____

3. What can you say to the driver? _____

_____

_____

_____

4. What can you say to Tim and Thang? _____

_____

5. Will you involve your principal? When? How? _____

_____

_____

_____

6. Will you involve any of the parents? When? How? _____

_____

_____

_____

Effects   What effects will your actions and responses have upon Manny?

_____

_____

_____

Tim and Thang? _____

_____

_____

The driver? _____

_____

_____

Your principal/school? _____

_____

_____

You? _____

_____

_____

Notes   _____

_____

_____

_____

_____

_____

Simulation 2.8 **While Rolling Along**

Setting:	On a school bus
Time:	In the afternoon, near the end of the school day
Persons involved:	Phil Stephens (a student from your school) and other pupils
Background information:	You don't know Phil. However, all of the students on your bus are from your school.
Circumstances:	Three busloads of pupils have been on a full-day field trip. You are the only chaperone on your bus. You've been sitting up front, exhausted from the day. Typical student noises are filtering to the front of the bus.
Simulation:	All of a sudden you realize that it has become very quiet on the bus. Then you hear some shrieks and laughter. You get up to investigate amid whispered "Teacher coming!" You see Phil jumping into his seat, zipping his zipper, and closing his belt. You say, "What's happening back here?" And someone shouts, "He dropped his pants!" The laughter and cheering begin again.

Reactions

1. What are you going to do? _____

_____

_____

_____

2. What will you say? _____

_____

_____

_____

3. Will you report the incident to the principal? Why? _____

_____

_____

_____

4. Will you talk to Phil privately when you get back to school? If yes, what will you say? If no, why? _____

_____

_____

5. How could you have prevented this event? _____

_____

_____

_____

Effects   What effects will your actions and responses have upon Phil?

_____

_____

_____

The other students? _____

_____

_____

_____

Your principal/school? _____

_____

_____

_____

You? _____

_____

_____

_____

Notes   _____

_____

_____

_____

_____

_____

_____

_____

_____

_____

Simulation 2.9 **Not a Funny Joke**

Setting:	Your classroom
Time:	At the start of a class period
Persons involved:	Cindy Lu Jones and Alice Hale (two of your students)
Background information:	Cindy Lu has never been in trouble. However, she is somewhat immature and she often likes to play jokes on people. Alice is a quiet, well-behaved student.
Circumstances:	Your students are just arriving for class. Cindy Lu has already taken her seat. Alice arrives and walks to her seat.
Simulation:	When Alice sits down she jumps, screams, and cries—all at once. You rush over and see Alice pulling a thumbtack from her behind. Cindy Lu is slouched down in her seat, looking guilty.

Reactions

1. What will you do for Alice? Say to Alice? _____

_____

_____

_____

2. How will you determine who put the tack on Alice's seat?

_____

_____

_____

3. If you determine that Cindy Lu put the tack on Alice's seat, what will you do? Say? _____

_____

_____

_____

4. If you can't determine who put the tack on Alice's seat, what will you do? Say? _____

_____

_____

_____

5. If you decide to lecture your class on hazards of practical jokes, what will you say? _____

_____

_____

_____

Effects What effects will your actions and responses have upon Alice?

_____

_____

_____

Cindy Lu? _____

_____

_____

_____

The other students? _____

_____

_____

_____

Your principal/school? _____

_____

_____

_____

You? _____

_____

_____

_____

Notes _____

_____

_____

_____

_____

Simulation 2.10 **In the Bushes**

Setting:	Outside of your school
Time:	After school
Person involved:	Saul Hudson (a student in your school)
Background information:	You have seen Saul before, but he has never been in your class. You did hear, in the teachers' lounge, that he has been in some trouble before.
Circumstances:	You are leaving school at the end of the day. You're walking down the sidewalk and you notice a person behind some bushes.
Simulation:	As you approach you see that the person is Saul and that he is urinating behind the bush.

Reactions

1. What are your options? _____

_____

_____

_____

2. Will you become involved? Why? _____

_____

_____

_____

3. If you do become involved, what will you say? _____

_____

_____

_____

4. Will you report this incident to the principal? Why? _____

_____

_____

_____

Effects What effects will your actions and responses have upon Saul?

_____

_____

Your principal/school? _____

_____

_____

_____

You? _____

_____

_____

_____

Notes _____

_____

_____

_____

_____

_____

_____

_____

_____

_____

Simulation 2.11 **Fire Drill Again**

Setting: Your school hallway

Time: During your free period

Person involved: Ella Adams (a student in your school)

Background information: You do not know Ella Adams.

Circumstances: Your school has been plagued by false fire alarms. The principal has discussed the problem with the entire student body and there have been no false alarms for about three weeks.

Simulation: You are walking down the hall toward the school office. As you turn a corner you notice a student fooling around with a hallway fire alarm box. Not seeing you, she pulls the alarm hook. As the bells begin to ring, she runs. As soon as she sees you, she turns around and runs the other way.

Reactions

1. What is your major objective? _____

_____

_____

_____

2. What will you do? _____

_____

_____

_____

3. If you catch the girl (Ella), what will you do? Say? _____

_____

_____

_____

4. If you don't catch Ella, what will you do? _____

_____

_____

_____

_____

Effects   What effects will your actions and responses have upon Ella?

_____

_____

_____

Your principal/school? _____

_____

_____

_____

You? _____

_____

_____

_____

Notes   _____

_____

_____

_____

_____

_____

_____

_____

Who's Telling the Truth?

Setting: Your classroom

Time: Near the end of a class period

Persons involved: Dorothy Jenkins, Steven McGray, and Dennis Mallory (three of your students) and the rest of the class

Background information: Steven is a pleasant, hard-working pupil who has never been in trouble. Dennis has exhibited behavior problems many times in the past. In fact, you have caught him cheating and lying on two different occasions.

Circumstances: All of your students have been engaged in an activity this period that required a great deal of movement around the room. Dorothy has just walked over to you and said, "My money is missing from my wallet." You ask, "Are you sure you had the money when you came in?" She says, "Yes."

Simulation: You stop the class activity and say, "Dorothy is missing some money. Does anyone have anything to say?" Someone shouts out, "Dennis took it!" Then Dennis says, "Oh no I didn't, I saw Steven take it!" Steven looks shocked.

Reactions

1. What are your options? _____

_____

_____

_____

2. What will you do? Say? _____

_____

_____

3. If no one confesses, what will you do? Say? _____

_____

_____

_____

4. Will you involve your principal? Why? _____

_____

_____

5. What can be done to reduce the chances of theft in your classroom? _____

_____

_____

_____

Effects What effects will your actions and responses have upon Dorothy?

_____

_____

_____

Steven? _____

_____

_____

_____

Dennis? _____

_____

_____

_____

Your principal/school? _____

_____

_____

_____

You? _____

_____

_____

_____

Notes _____

_____

_____

_____

_____

_____

Behavior Problems

Do you want to be respected and loved by your students? If so, you should be a very effective, creative teacher who puts a great deal of energy into helping students achieve. You will also need to be a person who creates and maintains an educational atmosphere that has few interruptions, disruptions, and behavior problems. If you are able to achieve these two goals you should gain the adoration of your students.

This chapter has offered you many ideas regarding the control and handling of unexpected behavior difficulties. You have also had a chance, through the pre-simulation exercises and actual role-play activities, to rehearse a variety of possible solutions to behavior problems. Your next step is to face the realities of a classroom and try your methods, approaches, and skills. Given your intelligence, teaching ability, and preparation via this chapter, you should be ready to handle a wide range of behavior problems.

Chapter 3

Health and Safety

Imagine yourself faced with a split-second life-or-death decision involving one of your pupils. Shudder at the thought? Extremely serious situations that are life-threatening occur only rarely. However, it is very important to be prepared, as you are the individual who has a legal and moral responsibility to react properly when such situations arise.

Most unexpected events that involve teachers are fairly minor and should be handled logically and easily. Some events require extreme care and immediate response. This chapter will give you opportunities to become better prepared for minor and serious events involving health and safety.

Factors to Consider

Six major factors deserve your consideration as you prepare to deal with the health and safety of your students. The factors include school policies, community services, health history, observation skills, first aid ability, and general precautions.

1. You should know your school's policy or approved plan of action for handling health and accident crises. Some schools may require that you invoke special procedures for only major problems. Other schools may have different systems for handling minor and major events.

You should know whom to contact in your school and how to reach that person. You also should know the chain of command in case your contact person, such as the school nurse or principal, is not available. The specific levels of authority should be clearly understood so that you know *who* is to do *what* in the event of an emergency.

2. Knowledge of your community's emergency medical services is imperative. Does your town use a 911 emergency

phone system? Should you call a hospital for assistance? How do you contact an ambulance or rescue squad? How long would it usually take for help to arrive? Consider these questions now and you'll be better prepared.

3. Health histories for all of your students should be available. You probably don't need to research every one of your pupils' health histories. It would be wise, however, to ask your school nurse or health aide to alert you to any problems among your students. You certainly should know if any of your pupils have health problems, such as a heart condition, diabetes, or epilepsy, that may require special precautions or actions in case of sudden illness or injury.

4. Your ability to accurately observe your students is another factor to consider as you prepare to deal with health and safety events. Observe such things as complexion, attention span, activity or energy level, and posture, and try to remember what is normal. Changes from the normal that are drastic and rapid probably need immediate attention. Slow and minor changes usually can be handled by a referral to the school nurse, counselor, or other appropriate personnel.

5. It is extremely wise for you to have current training and certification in first aid procedures. Such training would enable you to follow accepted practices when dealing with health emergencies. Courses in first aid are usually available without charge from your local American Red Cross. Many teachers have elected to take college-level first aid classes as part of their teacher certification programs.

6. Finally, be sure to consider the precautions that you can take to prevent injuries or health problems. Be sure to use good common sense whenever you are planning an activity in school or in the community. Consider safety and health first. It would be extremely unwise to plan and initiate any school activity that might cause risk to a student.

Think About It

These questions are presented to assist you as you begin thinking about unexpected events involving threats to health and safety. Discuss each of these questions with other members of your group. Then write the responses that you feel will help you be better prepared to handle unexpected health and safety problems. Sample responses are given in question 1.

1. What can you do to reduce the occurrence or severity of health and safety problems?

Plan all field trips carefully.

Use and store all school equipment and tools properly.

Wear, and have students wear, proper clothing for activities.

Consider the effects of heat and weather when outside.

Memorize or post the phone number of your community's emergency services.

Additional Responses:

_____

_____

_____

_____

2. What should you do and who should be contacted in your school if the following events were to occur? Write your responses in proper order. (If you are not

currently teaching, check the policy of one of your local schools.)

a. Student has a minor finger cut. _____

_____

_____

_____

_____

b. Student vomits. _____

_____

_____

_____

_____

c. Student collapses and stops breathing. _____

_____

_____

_____

_____

d. Student reports a fire in the next classroom. _____

_____

_____

_____

_____

Remember all of these events have happened to teachers and could happen to you. Preparation for these unexpected events is critical.

Simulations

It's now time to consider the actual simulations. Once you have responded to each of the simulations, your group or class should conduct the role-play activities.

Simulation 3.1 **To Breathe or Not to Breathe**

Setting:	Your classroom
Time:	During a regular teaching period
Persons involved:	Winnie Lee (one of your students) and the rest of your pupils
Background information:	Winnie Lee is a student with no known health problems.
Circumstances:	You have been involved in teaching the lesson for a few minutes. You notice that Winnie has unwrapped a large, hard candy.
Simulation:	Winnie begins to wave her hands. Then she grabs at her throat and with a horrified look she collapses to the floor. She is not breathing. A few of your students crowd around, others start to scream.

Reactions

1. What is your major objective? _____

_____

_____

_____

2. What will you do immediately? _____

_____

_____

_____

3. What other actions will you take? _____

_____

_____

_____

4. Do you feel responsible since you didn't stop Winnie from

eating the candy? Why? _____

_____

_____

_____

_____

5. How can you get your panicking students to become helpers?

_____

_____

_____

Effects   What effects will your actions and responses have upon Winnie?

_____

_____

_____

Your other students? _____

_____

_____

_____

Your principal/school? _____

_____

_____

_____

You? _____

_____

_____

_____

Notes   _____

_____

_____

_____

_____

_____

_____

_____

_____

Where There's Smoke There's Fire

Setting:	Your school hallway
Time:	Between classes
Persons involved:	Students in the hallway and in your classroom, and Mr. Archer, another teacher
Background information:	You teach in an old building. You have heard that there have been some problems with the incinerator.
Circumstances:	You are standing in the hall while students are arriving for their class with you.
Simulation:	As you turn to enter your classroom you notice some smoke coming into the hallway from a vent. You point out the smoke to Mr. Archer who says, "Oh, don't worry about it. It's probably just the old incinerator backed up again." He goes into his room and closes his door. Mr. Archer may be right, but you've never seen or smelled smoke before in your school.

Reactions

1. What is your primary objective? _____

_____

_____

_____

2. What are you going to do? In what order? _____

_____

_____

3. If you decided to ring the alarm and the smoke was from the "old incinerator," how will you respond to your principal? To

Mr. Archer? _____

_____

_____

_____

4. What can you do to prevent panic during a fire evacuation?

_____

_____

_____

Effects   What effects will your actions and responses have upon students? _____

_____

_____

_____

Mr. Archer? _____

_____

_____

_____

Your principal/school? _____

_____

_____

_____

You? _____

_____

_____

_____

Notes   _____

_____

_____

_____

_____

_____

_____

_____

_____

_____

Simulation 3.3 A Bloody Field Trip

Setting: A department store in your community

Time: During the day

Persons involved: Your entire class, Marshall Haupt (one of your students), and Mrs. Signor (a parent who volunteered to come with you)

Background information: You have taken your class on a field trip. You have obtained the necessary permission slips from all of your students' parents except for two. One is Marshall Haupt. And he's with you.

Circumstances: You and your class have just left the office of the store and are preparing to return to school.

Simulation: As you and your class are coming down the escalator, Marshall trips and falls. He has a bad cut on his scalp and his arm is in great pain. Your class crowds around, Mrs. Signor stands there looking frightened, and shoppers begin to stop and stare.

Reactions

1. What will you do first? _____

_____

_____

_____

2. What will your next actions be (in order)? _____

_____

_____

_____

3. How will you use Mrs. Signor? _____

_____

_____

_____

4. When will you tell your principal of the event? What will you say (if anything) about Marshall's lack of a permission slip?

_____

_____

_____

Effects   What effects will your actions and responses have upon
Marshall? _____

_____

_____

The students? _____

_____

_____

_____

Mrs. Signor? _____

_____

_____

_____

The store? _____

_____

_____

_____

Your principal/school? _____

_____

_____

_____

You? _____

_____

_____

_____

Notes   _____

_____

_____

_____

_____

_____

_____

_____

Simulation 3.4 **A Pill? A Drink?**

Setting: Your classroom

Time: During a regular teaching period

Persons involved: Agnes and Sylvia (two of your students) and the rest of your class

Background information: Agnes and Sylvia are usually well-behaved students. You've noticed that lately they have had difficulty concentrating on their work. The quality of their work has been dropping and their physical appearance suggests that they aren't getting enough sleep.

Circumstances: Agnes and Sylvia have just returned from the restroom.

Simulation: The two girls are unusually quiet and they both begin to fall asleep during class. Even after a bit of your scolding, they begin to sleep again.

Reactions

1. What are some of the possible causes for this sleeping behavior? _____

_____

_____

_____

2. What will you do? _____

_____

_____

_____

3. Will you notify anyone? Whom? When? How? _____

_____

_____

_____

4. What could you have done before so that this unexpected event would not have occurred? _____

_____

_____

_____

Effects   What effects will your actions and responses have upon Agnes and Sylvia? _____

_____

_____

_____

Your other students? _____

_____

_____

_____

Your principal/school? _____

_____

_____

_____

You? _____

_____

_____

_____

Notes   _____

_____

_____

_____

_____

_____

_____

_____

_____

_____

_____

Simulation 3.5 Out of the Sky

Setting:	Your classroom
Time:	During the school day
Persons involved:	Your students
Background information:	Before you arrived for work you heard that heavy storms were expected in your area that day.
Circumstances:	The skies have become extremely dark and a very heavy storm has begun. The power in the school has gone off, and the storm has become so severe that a few of your windows shatter and you can feel your building vibrating.
Simulation:	Your students begin to scream, cry, and panic.

Reactions
1. What will you do regarding the safety of your students and yourself? _____

_____

_____

_____

2. What will you do regarding panic? _____

_____

_____

_____

_____

3. What could your school have done before the storm to have reduced the crisis situation? _____

_____

_____

_____

4. What will you do after the storm is over? _____

_____

_____

_____

Effects   What effects will your actions and responses have upon your students? _____

_____

_____

_____

Your principal/school? _____

_____

_____

_____

You? _____

_____

_____

_____

Notes   _____

_____

_____

_____

_____

_____

_____

_____

Simulation 3.6 **Stranger in the Hall**

Setting:	Your classroom
Time:	During the school day
Persons involved:	A stranger (a young man who appears to be older than your students) and Angela (one of your students)
Background information:	Angela is one of your students who hangs around with a rough group of friends. You know that Angela's father has been in jail many times for a variety of offenses.
Circumstances:	You saw this stranger on your school grounds earlier in the day. His dress and age indicated to you that he was not one of your school's students.
Simulation:	The stranger knocks on the door, says he's a friend of Angela, and asks to speak with her. You look at Angela and she looks frightened. He walks into your room. You ask him to leave as he needs a pass from the office. But he refuses to leave. He insists on talking to Angela.

Reactions

1. What are your objectives? _____

_____

_____

_____

2. What are you going to do? To say? _____

_____

_____

3. If you need assistance from the office or police, in what ways can you summon help? _____

_____

_____

4. What could you have done before the event so that this problem would not have occurred? _____

_____

_____

Effects   What effects will your actions and responses have upon Angela?

_____

_____

_____

The stranger? _____

_____

_____

_____

Your principal/school? _____

_____

_____

_____

You? _____

_____

_____

_____

Notes   _____

_____

_____

_____

_____

_____

_____

_____

_____

_____

_____

Simulation 3.7 **Where Did He Go?**

Setting: A large park about twenty miles from your school

Time: 2:00 P.M.

Persons involved: Roberto (one of your students), the rest of your students, and Mrs. Thomas (a school bus driver)

Background information: Mrs. Thomas is a stubborn, uncooperative individual. Roberto has a severe case of diabetes. He has gone into diabetic shock twice while in school—but never in your class.

Circumstances: You have just completed a field trip. You must leave the park at 2:00 P.M. so that the students will arrive back at school in time to catch their buses home.

Simulation: While boarding the bus you discover that Roberto is missing. Mrs. Thomas is very anxious to leave because of her schedule. Your students begin shouting Roberto's name. After a five-minute search, you still haven't found Roberto.

Reactions

1. What is your primary objective? _____

_____

_____

_____

2. What are you going to do regarding Roberto? _____

_____

_____

3. What are you going to do regarding getting the rest of the students back to school in time to catch their buses? _____

_____

_____

_____

4. Are you going to notify the school? The police? Roberto's family? What will you say? _____

_____

_____

5. What could you have done so that this event would not have occurred? _____

_____

_____

_____

Effects   What effects will your actions and responses have upon Roberto?

_____

_____

_____

Your students? _____

_____

_____

_____

Mrs. Thomas? _____

_____

_____

_____

Your principal/school? _____

_____

_____

_____

You? _____

_____

_____

_____

Notes   _____

_____

_____

_____

_____

_____

Simulation 3.8 **Student in Crisis**

Setting: Your classroom

Time: During a regular teaching period

Persons involved: Susan Brady (one of your pupils) and the rest of your class

Background information: To the best of your knowledge, no one in your class has any health problems.

Circumstances: You are showing a movie to your class.

Simulation: While the movie is running, one of your students yells, "Hey, look!" Everyone turns around and sees that Susan has fallen to the floor and is in convulsions. Some of the students find the seizure to be funny, and a few students seem upset and frightened. Susan is unconscious, convulsing, and breathing.

Reactions

1. What will you do immediately? _____

_____

_____

_____

2. What else will you do? In what order? _____

_____

_____

_____

3. Look in an up-to-date first aid manual. What are the correct first aid procedures for seizures? _____

_____

_____

_____

4. If you find out that Susan's health problem was not new, will you take any action concerning the fact that you weren't informed? If so, what? _____

_____

_____

_____

5. How will you handle questions from your students about the event? _____

_____

_____

_____

Effects   What effects will your actions and responses have upon Susan?

_____

_____

_____

Your students? _____

_____

_____

_____

Your principal/school? _____

_____

_____

_____

You? _____

_____

_____

_____

Notes   _____

_____

_____

_____

_____

_____

_____

_____

_____

_____

Simulation 3.9 **To the Bone**

Setting:	In the school auditorium
Time:	During one of your classes
Persons involved:	Maria Molina and Sara Bowers (two of your pupils) and your other students
Background information:	You have a well-behaved, cooperative group of students.
Circumstances:	You have taken your class to the school auditorium for today's lesson. All of your students are sitting on the edge of the stage as you speak to them from the audience area. When you finish giving them directions for the activity, the students all quickly move to where they are to go.
Simulation:	A few students, including Maria, jump from the stage. As Maria jumps, a board loosens, and the back of her leg from the knee up is sliced open by a piece of metal used to attach lighting. The cut is deep and long, and the bleeding is severe. When Sara sees the blood she faints.

Reactions

1. What are your major objectives? _____

_____

_____

_____

2. What will you do for Maria? In what order? _____

_____

_____

3. What will you do for Sara? When? _____

_____

_____

_____

4. What will you say to Maria? (She can't see her injury.)

_____

_____

_____

5. How will you involve your other students? _____

_____

_____

_____

Effects What effects will your actions and responses have upon Maria?

_____

_____

_____

Sara? _____

_____

_____

_____

Your other students? _____

_____

_____

_____

Your principal/school? _____

_____

_____

_____

You? _____

_____

_____

_____

Notes _____

_____

_____

_____

_____

_____

Stomach Problems

Setting: Your classroom

Time: After lunch—during class

Persons involved: Skip Foster, Lionel Jones, and Barbara Meekin (three of your students)

Background information: Your class returned from lunch about thirty minutes ago.

Circumstances: Skip raised his hand a few minutes ago. He asked to go to the bathroom saying he didn't feel well. You suggested that he go to the nurse's office. But Skip said he didn't need to. You allowed him to go to the bathroom.

Simulation: A couple of minutes later Lionel vomits all over his desk. Then Barbara says she feels sick and she vomits. A quick glance around the room indicates to you that a number of other students are looking sick.

Reactions

1. What are some possible causes of these sudden illnesses?

   _____

   _____

   _____

2. What are you going to do? In what order? _____

   _____

   _____

   _____

3. Have you remembered Skip? What will you do about him?

   _____

   _____

   _____

4. How and when will you involve your principal and/or school nurse? _____

   _____

   _____

Effects What effects will your actions and responses have upon Skip, Lionel, and Barbara? _____

_____

_____

_____

The other students? _____

_____

_____

_____

Your principal/school? _____

_____

_____

_____

You? _____

_____

_____

_____

Notes _____

_____

_____

_____

_____

_____

_____

_____

_____

_____

Simulation 3.11 **Those Teeny Tiny Creatures**

Setting: Your classroom

Time: During a class

Persons involved: Your students

Background information: You read in the local newspaper that there has been a problem with head lice in some area schools.

Circumstances: During your lesson you have noticed that a number of your students have been scratching their heads. You decide to investigate.

Simulation: You walk over to one of your students who was scratching her head and say, "Itchy?" She says, "Yes, I don't know why." You take a look and, sure enough, you see a few tiny lice in her hair.

Reactions

1. What are you going to do? _____

_____

_____

_____

2. What will you say to your students if they ask about head lice?

_____

_____

_____

3. Will you involve the parents in the treatment? Or should home involvement be initiated by the school nurse? Why? _____

_____

_____

_____

4. How will you check and, if necessary, treat yourself? _____

_____

_____

_____

_____

Effects What effects will your actions and responses have upon your
students? _____

_____

_____

_____

Your principal/school? _____

_____

_____

_____

You? _____

_____

_____

_____

Notes _____

_____

_____

_____

_____

_____

_____

_____

Simulation 3.12 **Abandon Ship!**

Setting:	A school bus on a busy highway
Time:	During a school day
Persons involved:	About forty-five students, Mrs. Briggs (another teacher), and Mr. Rossen (the bus driver)
Background information:	You, Mrs. Briggs, and both of your classes are on a field trip. Mrs. Briggs is a timid individual who you believe is unable to cope with emergencies.
Circumstances:	You are riding along a busy four-lane road when the motor seems to die.
Simulation:	As Mr. Rossen brings the bus to a stop along the side of the highway, you see heavy smoke and flames coming from the front of the bus. Mrs. Briggs screams and the students start to do the same. You realize that you must take charge.

Reactions

1. What will you do to gain control of the situation? _____

_____

_____

_____

2. What actions will you take? What directions will you give? In

what order? _____

_____

_____

_____

3. Once everyone is off the bus, what will you do to insure their

safety? _____

_____

_____

4. Will you give Mr. Rossen help in fighting the fire? Why?

_____

_____

_____

Effects   What effects will your actions and responses have upon the students? _____

_____

_____

_____

Mrs. Briggs? _____

_____

_____

Mr. Rossen? _____

_____

_____

Your principal/school? _____

_____

_____

You? _____

_____

_____

_____

Notes   _____

_____

_____

_____

_____

_____

_____

_____

_____

_____

Health and Safety

The health and safety of your pupils is a major responsibility. As a teacher, you must be prepared to handle all types of unexpected health and safety emergencies.

Being skilled in first aid is one excellent way to be prepared. A college course, American Red Cross classes, or other recognized first aid courses are excellent ways for you to gain first aid knowledge and expertise. Once you become certified in first aid, be sure to pursue refresher courses to stay abreast of the newest and best techniques.

Avoiding health and safety problems is also important. Before you plan an activity, think of any threats to health or safety that might occur. Be sure that none of your school activities poses any danger or excessive stress to you, other school employees, or students.

When problems do occur, approach them calmly. If you become agitated, others may do the same. Act deliberately and calmly so that you and others know what you are doing and what they can do to help. Appropriate behavior will usually establish your authority and your ability to get others to help you.

Finally, realize that pupils will become ill and that accidents will happen. If you have done everything possible to avoid the health or safety emergency and if you handle an event calmly and properly, then the final outcome will probably be positive.

Chapter 4

Students' Personal Problems

Children and adolescents are great. They are energetic, enthusiastic individuals. Most of us in the teaching profession really like being around and working with youngsters. It just seems to be very enjoyable to share all of life's growing, maturing moments and help the children and adolescents progress toward adulthood.

But there are problems. And we teachers can become very involved professionally and emotionally with our students and their problems.

As a teacher, you will be faced with the frustrations, illnesses, divorces, deaths, and other problems that affect your students' lives. You may be called upon by your students to play the roles of confessor, parent, lawyer, police officer, minister, and friend.

You need to be ready to deal with your students' crises. This chapter will offer you numerous ideas and realistic simulations to help prepare yourself.

Factors to Consider

Most of us can probably think back and identify one or two very special teachers—ones we will cherish forever. These persons were probably ones who had excellent teaching skills and taught the subject matter well. Or they may have been teachers whom we admired because of their ability to understand and communicate with us.

Let's assume that you already have excellent teaching skills. Here are some guidelines to assist you in understanding and communicating with your students.

1. *Let your students know that you are interested in them*. Ask them questions about out-of-school activities and hobbies. Go to school events when your students participate.

2. *Show your students that you are a*

real person. Inform your students if you aren't feeling well, or share a personal problem with them. This will help them see you as a real person with feelings and problems—just like everyone else.

3. *Make time and space for students to talk to you.* Let your students know when and where you will be available to talk if they want. Just a few minutes a week for this may be all that is necessary.

4. *When a student wants to talk, talk.* No matter how busy you are, some problems just cannot wait. If you determine that the student's problem can wait, make an appointment to talk later. Then keep the appointment. If the problem can't wait, do not delay—talk.

5. *Be a good listener.* When a student has a problem, he or she doesn't usually want to hear about similar problems that you have had. The student wants to tell you about his or her problem.

6. *Don't show amusement or shock.* When a student feels that he or she really has a problem, laughter or a horrified look from you won't help. It is a good idea for a teacher to be ready for anything.

7. *Prove your interest.* When you are listening to a student's problem, sit or stand facing the child. Maintain good eye contact. And be sure to avoid interruptions such as taking phone calls or checking the time.

8. *Help the student solve the problem.* The student may need assistance in thinking of problem-solving options. Give that assistance but let the student choose the option. If you make the selection, you have failed to help. If the student selected an option but the problem continues, another option can be chosen without harm to your working relationship.

9. *Don't forget that your values, mor-* als, and standards may be different from those of the student and the student's family. Consider the student's situation and environment, and try to help the student cope in a way that is appropriate to him or her—not especially to you.

10. *Show continued interest in the problem.* After you discuss an issue with a student, it is a good idea to close the conversation with a statement such as this: "Keep me informed of your progress. I'm interested in knowing how things go for you."

11. *Be sure to not betray a student's trust and confidence.* If a student asks you to keep a secret, be honest immediately if you can't. Some issues, such as child abuse, may require your reporting the problem to the authorities. Other issues should be kept confidential, and if that is what is expected by the student, that is the way it should be.

12. *Try to develop good working relationships with your school's guidance counselor, psychologist, social worker, nurse, and principal.* These staff members can give you and your students excellent assistance. Use their skills and knowledge and you won't have to tackle problems in isolation. Be sure to involve the other professionals if a critical issue, such as a threat of suicide, is presented.

These are just a few factors to consider as you work with students' personal problems. They are only a start, however, as you, your ideas, and your personality play a very important role.

Think About It

Before you begin the pre-simulation exercises, it would be wise to consider two issues. What are the types of problems you may encounter, and what resources are available to assist you? Brainstorm these two questions. Then write your responses in the provided spaces. One response is provided for each question to help get you started.

1. What are some of the types of students' problems you may encounter?

    a. Problems regarding health

    b. _____

    c. _____

    d. _____

    e. _____

    f. _____

    g. _____

    h. _____

2. Name school and community resources that may be used for the above problems.

    a. School nurse and local health clinic

    b. _____

    c. _____

    d. _____

    e. _____

    f. _____

    g. _____

    h. _____

Simulations

Now you should be ready to face the students. The following pre-simulation exercises will help you prepare for the role-playing activities and for real-life situations.

Simulation 4.1 **It Was Just a Phone Call!**

Setting: Your classroom

Time: Early in the morning, before school

Person involved: Beth Tyler (one of your students)

Background information: One day last week you telephoned Mrs. Tyler to let her know that Beth had not been turning in her homework recently. Mrs. Tyler assured you that she would see to it that Beth had her homework done every day.

Circumstances: The day after you telephoned, Mrs. Tyler called to let you know that Beth would be out for a few days because of illness. As you are getting ready for your first-period class, you see Beth standing in the doorway of your classroom.

Simulation: You ask Beth if she's feeling better. She says yes and then breaks down crying. You go to her and ask her what's wrong. Between sobs she tells you that her mother beat her because of your phone call. Her mother had wanted to keep her out of school because of her bruised face.

Reactions

1. What are your objectives? _____

_____

_____

2. What will you say to Beth? Will you ask for more details?

_____

_____

_____

3. What else will you do about this problem? _____

_____

_____

_____

4. What school or community resources may be helpful?

_____

_____

_____

Effects What effects will your actions and responses have upon Beth?

_____

_____

_____

Mrs. Tyler? _____

_____

_____

_____

Your principal/school? _____

_____

_____

_____

You? _____

_____

_____

_____

Notes _____

_____

_____

_____

_____

_____

_____

_____

_____

_____

Simulation 4.2 **Body Image**

Setting: Your classroom

Time: During your free period

Person involved: Christopher Pell (one of your students)

Background information: Christopher is a studious youngster who does very well in school. He has always seemed to be very mature for his age.

Circumstances: Christopher has often talked to you about little problems. You have only had to listen before and he would solve his problems by talking about them.

Simulation: Christopher has just stopped in. He says, "You know, I really hate gym class." You ask why and he says, "Because we have to change into gym clothes and I hate taking my clothes off in front of the other guys."

Reactions

1. What are some possible solutions to Christopher's problem?

_____

_____

_____

_____

2. What will you say to Christopher? _____

_____

_____

_____

_____

3. Will you discuss this with the physical education teacher? If so, what will you say? If not, why? _____

_____

_____

_____

4. Will you contact Christopher's parents? Why? _____

_____

_____

_____

Effects What effects will your actions and responses have upon Christopher? _____

_____

_____

_____

Your principal/school? _____

_____

_____

_____

You? _____

_____

_____

_____

Notes _____

_____

_____

_____

_____

_____

_____

_____

_____

Simulation 4.3 **Wheels, No—Mouth, Yes**

Setting:	The school office
Time:	During lunch hour
Persons involved:	Clara Moffett (one of your students) and Frank Fielding (a guidance counselor)
Background information:	Clara is one of your students. She is confined to a wheelchair because of a physical handicap.
Circumstances:	You have just walked into the office to check your mailbox. You notice Clara speaking with Mr. Fielding. Clara has tears running down her cheeks. You decide to walk over and see if you can help.
Simulation:	You politely ask, "What's wrong?" Mr. Fielding says, "Clara is upset because she can't take art class next year." You respond with, "Why not?" Clara immediately replies, "Because of the XX$%#¢*& steps in this @#\#$X%%¢X% school!" Mr. Fielding says, "Why you dirty mouth kid," and he walks away.

Reactions   1. What are your objectives? _____

_____

_____

_____

2. What will you say to Clara? _____

_____

_____

_____

3. Will you go speak to Mr. Fielding? If so, what will you say? If

not, why? _____

_____

_____

4. How can you help solve Clara's problem? _____

_____

_____

5. How will you respond to Clara's cursing? _____

_____

_____

_____

Effects   What effects will your actions and responses have upon Clara?

_____

_____

_____

Mr. Fielding? _____

_____

_____

_____

Your principal/school? _____

_____

_____

_____

You? _____

_____

_____

_____

Notes   _____

_____

_____

_____

_____

_____

_____

_____

_____

_____

Simulation 4.4 **Not the Time or Place!**

Setting: Your classroom

Time: During the lunch period

Person involved: Robert Freeman (one of your students)

Background information: Robert is a quiet, rather withdrawn pupil. He does not socialize well with his peers, and he does not speak openly with you.

Circumstances: Robert asked you if he could sit in your classroom over the lunch hour so that he could do some reading. You said he may. When you left for lunch you said, "I'll see you in about a half hour." But when you got to the cafeteria you remembered you had brought your lunch. So you hurried back to your room to get it.

Simulation: When you walk into your room you find Robert looking at a dirty magazine and masturbating. He immediately stops and tries to hide what he was reading and doing.

Reactions

1. What are your options? _____

_____

_____

_____

2. Select your best option and explain why it is best. _____

_____

_____

_____

3. Select your second-best option and explain why it is second best. _____

_____

_____

4. What will you say to Robert with the above options?

Best option: _____

_____

_____

_____

Second-best option: _____

_____

_____

_____

5. Should this event be reported to the principal? Why?

_____

_____

_____

Effects   What effects will your actions and responses have upon Robert?

_____

_____

_____

Your principal/school? _____

_____

_____

_____

You? _____

_____

_____

_____

Notes   _____

_____

_____

_____

_____

_____

_____

_____

_____

Simulation 4.5 **Why Am I Different?**

Setting:	Your classroom
Time:	After school
Person involved:	Trevor McCardle (one of your students)
Background information:	Trevor is a special education student and is classified as educable mentally retarded. He seems to be very skilled in athletics. This year he has been mainstreamed into some regular classes.
Circumstances:	Trevor has seemed to be quite depressed lately. You've observed that he has not smiled once in class during the last week.
Simulation:	Trevor walks into your classroom to return a book he had borrowed. You say, "Trevor, you've looked pretty down lately. What's the problem?" He answers, "I just wish they'd leave me alone. Why aren't I like everyone else? Why do all the kids call me retard?"

Reactions

1. What do you know about mental retardation? _____

_____

_____

_____

2. What are your objectives? _____

_____

_____

_____

3. What will you say to Trevor? _____

_____

_____

_____

4. How else can you help Trevor? _____

_____

_____

_____

Effects   What effects will your actions and responses have upon Trevor?

_____

_____

_____

Other students? _____

_____

_____

_____

Your principal/school? _____

_____

_____

_____

You? _____

_____

_____

_____

Notes   _____

_____

_____

_____

_____

_____

_____

_____

_____

Simulation 4.6 **Invitation Time**

Setting:	A student restroom
Time:	During your free period
Persons involved:	Two students
Background information:	You do not know either of the two students involved in this event.
Circumstances:	You are hurrying to the school office as you are late for an appointment to see the assistant principal about a problem. As you pass by a student restroom you hear someone crying. A student walks out of the restroom and says to you, "Wow, someone in there sure is upset." The student walks away. You quickly consider your options: ignoring the problem, reporting the incident in the office, or going into the restroom to investigate. You choose the latter.
Simulation:	In the restroom you find a student crying hysterically. You ask, "What's wrong?" The student replies between sobs, "I wasn't invited to Melinda's party and everyone else was."

Reactions

1. What will you say to this student? _____
_____
_____
_____

2. Will you talk to anyone else about the student's problem? If so, who? What will you say? _____
_____
_____
_____

3. Will you try to find Melinda and talk to her? If yes, what will you say? If no, why? _____
_____
_____
_____
_____

4. What about your appointment? What will you tell the assistant principal? _____

_____

_____

_____

Effects   What effects will your actions and responses have upon the student? _____

_____

_____

_____

Melinda? _____

_____

_____

_____

Your principal/school? _____

_____

_____

_____

You? _____

_____

_____

_____

Notes   _____

_____

_____

_____

_____

_____

_____

_____

_____

Simulation 4.7 **Social Disease**

Setting: Your classroom

Time: Between classes

Persons involved: Doug Martin, Steve Smith, and Andy Brost (your students)

Background information: Doug, Steve, and Andy are very good friends. You have developed an excellent rapport with the three of them.

Circumstances: Doug, Steve, and Andy come by to talk to you. Doug informs you that there's a problem they'd like to discuss, so you invite them into your room. Andy looks very nervous.

Simulation: You start the conversation with, "So what's on your minds, boys?" Doug and Steve do all of the talking and tell you that Andy thinks he has VD. You ask Andy why he thinks he has VD and he says, "Because it burns when I urinate."

Reactions

1. What are some of the symptoms of VD? _____

_____

_____

_____

2. What are your objectives? _____

_____

_____

_____

3. What will you say to the boys? _____

_____

_____

_____

4. What will you recommend to Andy? _____

_____

_____

_____

_____

5. Will you report this information to Andy's parents? Why? To the school nurse? Why? _____

_____

_____

_____

Effects What effects will your actions and responses have upon Andy?

_____

_____

_____

Doug and Steve? _____

_____

_____

_____

Your principal/school? _____

_____

_____

_____

You? _____

_____

_____

_____

Notes _____

_____

_____

_____

_____

_____

_____

_____

_____

_____

Simulation 4.8 Homosexuality

Setting:	Your classroom
Time:	Before school
Person involved:	Tina Sheldon (one of your students)
Background information:	You have known Tina for a few years. She is a very good student and you and she communicate well. You are also close friends with Mrs. Sheldon, Tina's mother.
Circumstances:	Tina steps into your room and asks if you're busy. You say, "Never too busy to talk to you." Her response is "Well this is kind of heavy—I just don't know who to talk to." So you sit down, ask Tina to sit down, and say, "Go ahead, talk, I'm your friend."
Simulation:	Tina says, "I think I'm gay. I've had sex with an older girl. Oh, I don't know what to do!" And Tina begins to cry.

Reactions

1. Why would it be unwise to be strongly pro-gay in your talk with Tina? _____

_____

_____

_____

2. Why would it be unwise to be strongly anti-gay in your talk with Tina? _____

_____

_____

_____

3. What will you say to Tina? _____

_____

_____

_____

4. Is a referral to a counselor needed? Why? _____

_____

_____

_____

5. Should you tell Mrs. Sheldon? Why? _____

_____

_____

_____

Effects   What effects will your actions and responses have upon Tina?

_____

_____

_____

Mrs. Sheldon? _____

_____

_____

_____

Your principal/school? _____

_____

_____

_____

You? _____

_____

_____

_____

Notes   _____

_____

_____

_____

_____

_____

_____

_____

_____

Simulation 4.9 Grass—And Not the Kind You Mow

Setting: A park in your community

Time: On a Saturday afternoon

Person involved: Billy Carver (a student you had in your class a few years ago)

Background information: Billy comes from a broken home in a very poor neighborhood of your town. He was a very poor student when he was in your class. He also skipped school a great deal and got himself into trouble often.

Circumstances: You're walking through the park with some friends. Billy walks by and says hello. You recognize him and say, "Well how have you been? What are you up to these days?"

Simulation: Billy's response is, "Oh, everything is OK. Say, I figure you're pretty with it so—well—would you want to buy some grass?" And Billy produces a small package of marijuana for your inspection. One of your friends asks, "How much?"

Reactions

1. What are your objectives? _____

_____

_____

2. What will you say to Billy? _____

_____

_____

3. What will you say to your friends? _____

_____

_____

4. Will you report this incident to the police? Why? _____

_____

_____

5. Will you report this incident to your principal? Why?

_____

_____

_____

Effects What effects will your actions and responses have upon Billy?

_____

_____

_____

Your friends? _____

_____

_____

_____

Your principal/school? _____

_____

_____

_____

You? _____

_____

_____

_____

Notes _____

_____

_____

_____

_____

_____

_____

_____

_____

_____

Eyes? No. Ears? No. Nose? Yes.

Setting:	Your classroom
Time:	During class
Persons involved:	Martha Rodgers and a few of your other students sitting near her
Background information:	Martha is a quiet student who doesn't seem to have any friends. Her clothing never looks clean and you have noticed that on some days she has an unpleasant body odor.
Circumstances:	You have just assigned numbers to your students so they can move into groups for the next activity. Two of your students, who were supposed to sit with Martha, refuse to sit down. You walk over to see what is wrong.
Simulation:	You ask, "What's the matter?" Both girls whisper to you that they don't want to sit with Martha because she smells. Martha immediately begins to cry. You ask her why she's crying and she says, "Because everyone hates me!"

Reactions

1. What are your objectives? _____

_____

_____

_____

2. What will you say to Martha? _____

_____

_____

_____

3. What will you say to the girls who wouldn't sit with Martha?

_____

_____

_____

4. What can you do to help Martha overcome this problem?

_____

_____

_____

5. Will you report this problem to anyone else? To whom?

_____

_____

_____

Effects   What effects will your actions and responses have upon Martha?

_____

_____

_____

The other students? _____

_____

_____

_____

Your principal/school? _____

_____

_____

_____

You? _____

_____

_____

Notes   _____

_____

_____

_____

_____

_____

_____

_____

_____

_____

This Isn't a Joke

Setting:	Your classroom
Time:	After class
Person involved:	Mickey Wilkins (one of your students)
Background information:	Mickey's mother died three weeks ago after a very long illness. Mr. Thomas, Mickey's stepfather, is known for his drinking and violent temper.
Circumstances:	Mickey returned to school two weeks ago, the day after his mother's funeral. He seemed to be readjusting until the past few days when he became deeply sullen. Today he looks exhausted and depressed. While the rest of the students were working, you asked Mickey if he would like to talk to you after class. He said, "Yes."
Simulation:	After class, you say to Mickey, "Would you like to talk about what's bothering you? Maybe I can help." Mickey says, "My stepfather has started drinking again and he hit me last night for nothing. I can't stand living anymore. Maybe I'll just join my Mom." And then Mickey just stares off into space.

Reactions

1. What do you think Mickey is trying to tell you? _____

_____

_____

_____

2. What are your objectives? _____

_____

_____

3. What are you going to say to Mickey? _____

_____

_____

4. Will you involve others in this problem? Who and when?

_____

_____

_____

5. How can you help Mickey over the next days and weeks?

_____

_____

_____

Effects What effects will your actions and responses have upon Mickey?

_____

_____

_____

Mr. Thomas? _____

_____

_____

_____

Your principal/school? _____

_____

_____

_____

You? _____

_____

_____

_____

Notes _____

_____

_____

_____

_____

_____

_____

_____

_____

Simulation 4.12 Can't Tell My Parents

Setting:	Your classroom
Time:	During your lunch break
Person involved:	Amy Michaels (one of your former students)
Background information:	Amy was a delightful student. Since leaving your classroom, she has often come by to visit you. Both of you interact quite well, and you have been comfortable discussing some of her personal life, such as her future hopes and her present dating experiences.
Circumstances:	Amy telephoned you yesterday and said she was having a problem. She asked if she could come by and see you today. You suggested that the two of you meet during your lunch hour.
Simulation:	After an exchange of greetings you say, "Well, what's been bothering you?" Amy's reply is, "I think I'm pregnant. I don't know what to do. My parents will probably throw me out of the house."

Reactions

1. What are your objectives? _____

_____

_____

_____

2. What will you say? _____

_____

_____

_____

3. What resources can you suggest? _____

_____

_____

_____

4. Should you report this to your principal? Why? _____

_____

_____

_____

5. Should you contact Amy's parents? Why? _____

_____

_____

_____

Effects   What effects will your actions and responses have upon Amy?

_____

_____

_____

Your principal/school? _____

_____

_____

_____

You? _____

_____

_____

_____

Notes   _____

_____

_____

_____

_____

_____

_____

_____

_____

_____

Students' Personal Problems

You have just had an opportunity to experience a number of simulations of unexpected events that involve students and their problems. Some of the difficulties can be handled quickly and easily while others can cause great frustration and concern.

Are you ready for events like these? Realize that you may be called upon to help students solve problems that appear grave to them. Your reactions, gestures, expressions, and comments will all be digested and interpreted by the students. It is therefore extremely important for you to think first and react in a calm, unbiased manner. Involve your principal or other professionals if necessary. And be sure to keep lines of communication open between you and your students.

Chapter 5

Dealing with Parents

Your preparation for dealing with the unexpected began with the consideration of events directly involving your pupils. The exercises and simulations in this chapter offer you an opportunity to think about and prepare for the many types of parent interactions you may someday face.

Teachers are repeatedly involved in unexpected interactions with parents and guardians. It is extremely important to you to be able to handle these events calmly and rationally so that you can protect yourself from harm or legal action. You will also want to preserve or develop a positive rapport with the parents for future cooperation.

A variety of factors influence and motivate parents. You will be asked to consider those factors and to think about appropriate ways of dealing with parents. Then you will have an opportunity to sample and role-play a number of real-life occurrences involving teachers and parents.

Factors to Consider

As you think about the many and varied types of events that may involve parents, it is important for you to reflect upon such factors as the history of parent interactions with the school, your previous experiences with the parents, and the present emotional, economic, social, employment, and marital status of the parents. You should watch for clues or behaviors that suggest the parents' present emotional status. It is naturally impossible, and perhaps inappropriate, for you to know everything, but some knowledge of these factors should help you decide what to say and what to do. Any prior knowledge of and thought about your students' parents and guardians may help you avoid uncomfortable and potentially dangerous problems.

It is also extremely important for you to consider the consequences of your own reactions, responses, expressions, and other behaviors. Before you initiate an action, try to predict what the parents may do or how they may feel because of your actions and statements. If you make a conscious effort to anticipate such consequences, you probably will be able to control the parents more easily in the situations presented.

The following are just a few guidelines that should assist you in dealing with parents:

1. *Do whatever is appropriate to know your students' parents.* Go on home visits. Talk by phone. Invite them to school.

2. *Always have something positive to say.* Be sure to tell the parents about something their children did well. Then you can discuss the problem.

3. *Call the parents when something is going well.* If you call just to congratulate occasionally, then your name or voice won't be associated with some negative condition.

4. *Let the parents know that you are sincerely interested in the progress being made by their children.* Share growth, problems, and teaching strategies so the parents are kept informed of what you are trying to do.

5. *Involve the parents.* Whenever possible seek their assistance and form a partnership for a common goal—the improvement of their children.

6. *When parents are upset, give them a chance to calm down.* Indicate to upset parents who have telephoned that you have a class or an appointment and call back in a few minutes. Or have upset parents who have come to school wait in the office a few minutes before you see them. This cooling-off period may be very helpful.

7. *Don't meet with parents who are the least bit upset in an isolated area of the school.* Have your meeting or conference in the office area. And have another professional with you if at all possible.

8. *Don't try to be everything to parents.* Remember, you are the teacher. There are other trained professionals—principals, counselors, social workers, and others who can provide assistance. Do what you can but don't hesitate to refer.

Think About It

Here are two questions to get you started as you mentally prepare to handle unexpected events related to the parents and guardians of your students. Consider each question and the sample responses. Then brainstorm each question, with other persons if possible, and evaluate the sample answers. Provide additional responses that you believe are appropriate and potentially helpful.

1.   What types of information should you know about your students' parents and guardians?

The ages of the parents

Their religious convictions

Educational levels of the parents

The ages of the other children in the house

Any history of child abuse

_____

_____

_____

_____

_____

2. What general rules can you adopt to help keep interactions with parents positive?

Stay calm or at least appear calm.

Listen carefully to what parents have to say.

Don't meet in isolated areas of the school.

Say something positive about the child.

Don't put down parents.

_____

_____

_____

_____

_____

Simulations

You are now ready for the pre-simulation exercises. Read the simulation descriptions and respond in the spaces provided.

Remember, be thorough as you complete the exercises. A few extra moments of thought now may help you avoid a terrible experience later.

After you have considered each of the simulations, you will be ready for group role-playing and reactions to the handling of the simulations by the assigned "teachers."

Mom Is Angry!

Setting:	Your classroom
Time:	During lunch period
Person involved:	Andy Perkins's mother (Andy is one of your students.)
Background information:	Mrs. Perkins has been to your school many times before. She has often complained about the school and, on numerous occasions, has demanded to talk to the principal. You heard from Andy that Mr. and Mrs. Perkins have separated.
Circumstances:	You sent a note home to Andy's parents advising them that Andy was being referred to the school psychologist because of his poor behavior in your class.
Simulation:	You are alone in your room, sitting at your desk eating lunch and grading papers. Mrs. Perkins bursts into your classroom screaming that Andy is not mentally ill and that you're ruining her marriage. She begins sobbing and using foul language.

Reactions

1. What would you do first? Why? _____

_____

_____

_____

2. What else would you do? Why? _____

_____

_____

_____

3. What should you consider in terms of protecting yourself and

the school? _____

_____

_____

4. Do you think a note home was a good idea? What else could

you have done? _____

_____

_____

Effects   What effects will your actions and responses have upon Andy?

_____

_____

_____

Mrs. Perkins? _____

_____

_____

Your principal/school? _____

_____

_____

You? _____

_____

_____

_____

Notes   _____

_____

_____

_____

_____

_____

_____

_____

_____

_____

_____

What's in the Lesson?

Setting:	Your principal's office
Time:	During your planning period
Persons involved:	Mr. Sanchez (father of Juan, one of your students) and Ms. Carter (school principal)
Background information:	The Sanchezes are new in your community and Juan has only been in your classes for two weeks. You have never met Mr. Sanchez.
Circumstances:	Ms. Carter just called your room and asked you to come to the office. She informed you that Mr. Sanchez was there. You have gone to the office, met Mr. Sanchez, and have taken a seat next to him.
Simulation:	Ms. Carter explains to you that Mr. Sanchez is concerned about your ability to teach since he doesn't think the information you are presenting in your classes is accurate and up-to-date. Mr. Sanchez states, in very difficult to understand English, that this is his major concern. Ms. Carter doesn't come to your defense. She simply asks for your response.

Reactions

1. What will you say to Mr. Sanchez? _____
   _____
   _____

2. What will you say to Ms. Carter? _____
   _____
   _____

3. How do you feel about Mr. Sanchez's accusations? _____
   _____
   _____
   _____

4. How do you feel about Ms. Carter's handling of the situation?
   _____
   _____
   _____

Effects   What effects will your actions and responses have upon Mr.
Sanchez? _____

_____

_____

_____

Ms. Carter? _____

_____

_____

Juan? _____

_____

_____

You? _____

_____

_____

Notes   _____

_____

_____

_____

_____

_____

_____

_____

_____

_____

Simulation 5.3 Grading—What a Headache!

Setting: Your classroom

Time: Early morning, before school has started

Persons involved: Sally Schmid (one of your students), Mrs. Schmid, and two other students

Background information: Sally is a bright pupil. She is strongly motivated to achieve due to extreme parental pressure. You have often worried about the effects of the parents' pressure.

Circumstances: Report cards were distributed yesterday. Although Sally's work in your class was excellent and A level (as usual), it was consistently late and sloppy. Therefore, you decided that a B grade was appropriate.

Simulation: You are alone, working at the chalkboard, when Mrs. Schmid storms into your room dragging a crying Sally along. When you ask what is wrong, Mrs. Schmid begins to loudly and strongly accuse you of unfair grading practices. She indicates that you are ruining Sally's excellent school record and that you are not emphasizing the proper thing—the quality and content of Sally's work. Two of your students walk into your room and overhear Mrs. Schmid's complaints.

Reactions

1. What will you say/do to help calm Mrs. Schmid? _____

_____

_____

_____

2. What will you say in response to Mrs. Schmid's complaint?

_____

_____

_____

3. Will you involve Sally? How? _____

_____

_____

_____

_____

4. What will you say/do in regard to the two other students who walked into your room? _____

_____

_____

5. Do you think that teachers should lower a grade because of lateness and/or sloppiness? Why? _____

_____

_____

Effects   What effects will your actions and responses have upon Sally?

_____

_____

_____

Mrs. Schmid? _____

_____

_____

The other students? _____

_____

_____

Your principal/school? _____

_____

_____

You? _____

_____

_____

Notes   _____

_____

_____

_____

_____

Simulation 5.4 **A Divorce—A Decision**

Setting:	Your classroom
Time:	During a regularly scheduled parent conference
Persons involved:	Mr. and Mrs. Kaplan (parents of Anna, one of your students)
Background information:	Mr. and Mrs. Kaplan have been supportive, pleasant parents whom you have come to know quite well, or so you thought.
Circumstances:	The Kaplans asked for this conference to discuss a problem they are having.
Simulation:	After briefly discussing Anna's good performance in your class, Mr. Kaplan tells you that they have a very serious problem and they would appreciate your advice. When you agree to listen, they indicate that they have decided to get a divorce. Their concern is with whom Anna should live. They each want Anna and Anna doesn't know what to do. So she told her parents she would go with the one *you* recommend. They then ask for your recommendation.

Reactions 1. What will you say? Why? _____

_____

_____

2. To whom can you refer the Kaplans for additional assistance?

_____

_____

_____

3. When the Kaplans indicated that they have a serious problem, should you have agreed to listen? Why? _____

_____

_____

_____

Effects   What effects will your actions and responses have upon Mr. and Mrs. Kaplan? _____

_____

_____

Anna? _____

_____

_____

_____

Your principal/school? _____

_____

_____

_____

You? _____

_____

_____

Notes   _____

_____

_____

_____

_____

_____

_____

_____

_____

Simulation 5.5 **A Special Education Label**

Setting:	Your school hallway
Time:	In the evening, during school open house
Person involved:	Mrs. Chester (mother of Stanley, one of your pupils)
Background information:	Stanley, a pupil who has demonstrated excellent athletic ability, is a learning-disabled student who has been mainstreamed into your class. Mrs. Chester is divorced and is raising four children on her own. You have never met Mrs. Chester.
Circumstances:	The school open house is an informal program for parents to drop in and chat. Mrs. Chester stops to talk to you.
Simulation:	You go through appropriate introductions and indicate that it's good to see Mrs. Chester and that you have time to talk. Mrs. Chester immediately begins to tell you all her financial troubles and some rather personal problems. She indicates that Stanley hates school and that she doesn't blame him because many of his friends kid him by calling him "reject" and "retard" since he is in a learning disability program. She also tells you that Stanley's siblings make fun of him because of his difficulty with schoolwork.

Reactions

1. What do you want to accomplish as you talk with Mrs. Chester? _____

_____

_____

_____

2. What will you say to her? _____

_____

_____

3. What suggestions will you make regarding Stanley's friends? Stanley's siblings? _____

_____

_____

4. What other school resources might you involve? _____

_____

_____

_____

Effects   What effects will your actions and responses have upon Mrs.
Chester? _____

_____

_____

Stanley? _____

_____

_____

Your principal/school? _____

_____

_____

You? _____

_____

_____

Notes   _____

_____

_____

_____

_____

_____

_____

_____

_____

_____

A Disastrous Home Visit

Setting:	The home of one of your pupils
Time:	About 4:30 P.M. on a school day
Persons involved:	Mr. and Mrs. Copeland (parents of Susan, one of your students)
Background information:	Mrs. Copeland has often been to school and has appeared to be a supportive, interested parent. You have never discussed Mr. Copeland with her. Susan has not said anything about the problem.
Circumstances:	You have heard rumors from a couple of your students that Mr. Copeland has been physically abusing Susan. You decided to stop by their house just to say hello and get a "feel" for the situation.
Simulation:	When you arrive, you are greeted by Mrs. Copeland. Although surprised to see you, she promptly invites you in. After a brief conversation you ask Mrs. Copeland how Susan and Mr. Copeland get along. You learn from Mrs. Copeland that her husband has a bad temper. Mr. Copeland arrives, obviously drunk, and loudly tells you to get out of their house and to quit butting into their business.

Reactions

1. What will you do first? Why? _____

_____

_____

2. What will you say to Mrs. Copeland? Mr. Copeland?

_____

_____

_____

3. What will you do about the situation after you leave?

_____

_____

_____

_____

4. Do you think you should have gone to the Copeland's home? At all? Alone? Without an appointment? _____

_____

_____

_____

Effects   What effects will your actions and responses have upon Mrs. Copeland? _____

_____

_____

_____

Mr. Copeland? _____

_____

_____

_____

Susan? _____

_____

_____

_____

Your principal/school? _____

_____

_____

_____

You? _____

_____

_____

_____

Notes _____

_____

_____

_____

_____

Simulation 5.7 **A Difference in Race**

Setting:	The parking lot of a local supermarket
Time:	Saturday afternoon
Persons involved:	Annette Fagen (one of your students), Mrs. Fagen, and one of Mrs. Fagen's friends, Mrs. Knight
Background information:	Annette has consistently been doing very poorly in your class. Her last report card was especially bad. You have never met Mrs. Fagen or Mrs. Knight. You are of a different race than the two women.
Circumstances:	You have just finished doing your shopping and are putting your groceries in the car.
Simulation:	Mrs. Fagen, Mrs. Knight, and Annette walk over to you on the parking lot. Mrs. Fagen looks furious and she begins to yell at you for being unfair to her child because of her race. Mrs. Fagen's friend joins in and calls you a "racist" while Annette stands there and cries.

Reactions

1. If the situation makes you fear for your safety, what will you say and do? _____

_____

_____

2. If you are not in fear for your safety, what will you say and do?

_____

_____

_____

3. Will you involve Annette? How? _____

_____

_____

4. What can you do to reduce the chances of prejudice-type complaints or criticisms? _____

_____

_____

_____

Effects   What effects will your actions and responses have upon Mrs.
Fagen? _____

_____

_____

_____

Annette? _____

_____

_____

_____

Mrs. Fagen's friend? _____

_____

_____

_____

Your principal/school? _____

_____

_____

_____

You? _____

_____

_____

_____

Notes   _____

_____

_____

_____

_____

_____

_____

_____

_____

_____

_____

Simulation 5.8 **Whose Fault Was It?**

Setting: Your classroom

Time: During a parent conference

Persons involved: Mr. and Mrs. Harvey (parents of Sybil, one of your pupils)

Background information: Sybil is one of your students who has emotional problems. She is a bright pupil, but because of her unpredictable behaviors, she is not well liked by her peers. Most teachers in the school do not want Sybil in their classes since she tends to cause trouble. You have met with the Harveys before without any unexpected occurrences.

Simulation: The Harveys and you briefly discuss Sybil's slow school progress. Then Mr. Harvey raises the issue that Sybil's problems have been caused by Mrs. Harvey's side of the family. This begins a loud argument between the two parents about which parent caused Sybil's difficulties. It appears that the argument may become violent.

Reactions

1. What are you going to do/say immediately? _____

_____

_____

_____

2. Assuming that you have been able to calm down the parents, what will you say to them? _____

_____

_____

3. If you have not been able to calm down the parents, what will you do? _____

_____

_____

4. To what school resources and community agencies can you refer the Harveys? _____

_____

_____

Effects   What effects will your actions and responses have upon the
Harveys? _____

_____

_____

_____

Sybil? _____

_____

_____

_____

Your principal/school? _____

_____

_____

_____

You? _____

_____

_____

_____

Notes   _____

_____

_____

_____

_____

_____

_____

_____

_____

_____

_____

Late One Night

Setting: Your bedroom

Time: Approximately 11:30 P.M.

Person involved: Mrs. Jegerski (widowed mother of Alan, one of your students)

Background information: Alan's father passed away about three months ago. Since then Mrs. Jegerski has called you often about little problems. Although the calls have been somewhat annoying, you have graciously helped. You have asked her not to call you at home.

Circumstances: Alan has told you that his mother cries almost every night about his father's death.

Simulation: You are awakened by a phone call. After much coaxing you find out that the caller, who is crying, is Mrs. Jegerski. Alan has run away, she's frightened, is considering suicide, is begging you to come to her home.

Reactions

1. Are you going to go to Alan's home? Why? _____

_____

_____

_____

2. What will you say to Mrs. Jegerski? _____

_____

_____

_____

3. What agencies, if any, will you involve? When? How?

_____

_____

_____

4. Assuming that Alan will return, what will you say to him when you see him? _____

_____

_____

_____

5. Could you have avoided this phone call? How? _____

_____

_____

_____

Effects   What effects will your actions and responses have upon Mrs.
Jegerski? _____

_____

_____

_____

Alan? _____

_____

_____

_____

Your principal/school? _____

_____

_____

_____

You? _____

_____

_____

_____

Notes   _____

_____

_____

_____

_____

_____

_____

_____

_____

Simulation 5.10 **So That's Where It Comes From!**

Setting: Your classroom

Time: After school

Persons involved: Mr. Kent (foster father of Tanya, one of your pupils)

Background information: Mr. and Mrs. Kent serve as foster parents for a number of children. You have spoken to Mrs. Kent before but you have never met Mr. Kent.

Circumstances: You asked Mrs. Kent to come in to see you about a problem you have been having with Tanya—excessive cursing. You have heard that another child the Kents are raising has the same problem.

Simulation: Mr. Kent arrives to speak with you since Mrs. Kent is at home ill. He seems nervous while you tell him about Tanya's cursing problem. When he has a chance to respond, he apologizes and exclaims, "When I get the #$%@¢&XX home, I'll beat the @#○ $%¢&*X#$ out of the XX$%¢&@#* kid for not being good in school."

Reactions

1. How do you feel toward Mr. Kent? _____

_____

_____

2. Apparently Tanya has learned some cursing from Mr. Kent. Are you going to discuss this with him? If so, what will you say?

_____

_____

3. If you won't discuss this problem with Mr. Kent, what will you do? _____

_____

_____

_____

4. What options do you have for reducing Tanya's cursing behavior? _____

_____

_____

_____

Effects What effects will your actions and responses have upon Mr. Kent? _____

_____

_____

_____

Tanya? _____

_____

_____

_____

The Kent's other foster children? _____

_____

_____

_____

Your principal/school? _____

_____

_____

_____

You? _____

_____

_____

_____

Notes _____

_____

_____

_____

_____

Simulation 5.11 **Attendance Is Required**

Setting: School office—telephone area

Time: After school

Person involved: Mrs. Washington (mother of Dorothy, one of your students)

Background information: Mrs. Washington is a single parent who is raising three children. She works during the day and is not able to supervise them closely. Since school started this year, Dorothy has missed school at least two days each week.

Circumstances: You have reported the attendance problem to your principal, who indicated that the school district's social worker was advised. But you have decided to telephone Mrs. Washington yourself.

Simulation: You call Mrs. Washington and identify yourself. She immediately blames you for having someone from the school come by to embarrass and threaten her with legal action. She also says she has to work and can't know if her kids skip school.

Reactions

1. What will you say regarding the "blame" placed on you?

_____

_____

_____

2. What will you say about Dorothy's attendance? _____

_____

_____

_____

3. What can you do/say to help improve the entire situation?

_____

_____

_____

4. Should you have made this phone call? Why? _____

_____

_____

_____

Effects   What effects will your actions and responses have upon Mrs.
Washington? _____

_____

_____

_____

Dorothy? _____

_____

_____

_____

Your principal/school? _____

_____

_____

_____

You? _____

_____

_____

_____

Notes   _____

_____

_____

_____

_____

_____

_____

_____

_____

_____

_____

Simulation 5.12 **That Wonderful Bus**

Setting:	School office—telephone area
Time:	During a free period
Persons involved:	Mr. Tong (father of Duyen, one of your students)
Background information:	Duyen is an excellent student. You have met his parents and they are interested, supportive individuals. The Tongs have just moved from their home two blocks from the school to one three miles away. Duyen now must ride a school bus every day. You know from school rumors that there are often behavior problems on the school bus.
Circumstances:	You had a note in your mailbox to please call Mr. Tong.
Simulation:	After a brief exchange of greetings over the phone, Mr. Tong tells you that he is very upset. His reason is that "on the school bus there is some fighting, cursing, and smoking of cigarettes and marijuana." He asks you if you know about the problems and what you will do about them.

Reactions

1. Should you admit that you have heard that there are problems on the buses? Why? What will you say? _____

_____

_____

_____

2. What will you say regarding the solving of the problems?

_____

_____

_____

3. Will you involve your principal? How? _____

_____

_____

4. Will you talk to Duyen about the problem? Why? What will you say? _____

_____

_____

Effects   What effects will your actions and responses have upon Mr.
Tong? _____

_____

_____

_____

Duyen? _____

_____

_____

Your principal/school? _____

_____

_____

_____

You? _____

_____

_____

_____

Notes   _____

_____

_____

_____

_____

_____

_____

_____

_____

_____

Dealing with Parents

You've now had the opportunity to deal with just a few unexpected problems you may someday face as you interact with your pupils' parents and guardians. It is quite important for you to remember your role, to be concerned about your students, and to protect yourself from legal action and physical harm.

As a teacher you should be able to stay calm and cool and react in a professional manner. You represent your school, and your actions and statements may be subjected to close scrutiny by your peers and superiors. Reacting appropriately should protect you and your school from legal problems.

You naturally want to do what is best for the student involved. Immediate consequences and long-term effects must be considered before you act. Remember, you will probably continue to work with that student and the student's parents or guardians.

It is imperative for you to be concerned with your own health and safety. Avoiding meetings with parents in isolated areas of the school and taking another person with you on home visits are both good practices. Always think about yourself when unexpected events occur and try to avoid becoming a statistic.

There are many benefits to be gained from developing good, open communication lines between the parents and yourself, whether you are working with young children or adolescents. You will find great value in cooperation with parents.

It is important to realize that most parents and guardians are caring, pleasant individuals who want to work well with you. Encourage and support these parents and perhaps you can involve them in helping the others.

Chapter 6

The Rest of the Staff

Teachers certainly don't work in a vacuum. They must work with administrators and supervisors from their own school as well as the school district. Teachers interact with personnel such as office staff, other teachers, librarians, custodians, bus drivers, school nurses, guidance counselors, cafeteria workers, teachers' aides, coaches, music directors, and volunteers. The collective influence that these other school employees have on a teacher is great. Therefore, it behooves every teacher to attempt to work well with the other personnel, respect them for their contributions, and avoid or reduce the impact of unexpected events.

Factors to Consider

As you work with other members of the school staff, you need to keep in mind the following:

1. These persons should have goals similar to yours regarding the provision of a sound educational program.

2. These persons have particular skills and/or knowledge that you may not possess.

3. Some of these persons answer to different supervisors who may not communicate well or agree with your boss.

4. These persons are influenced by their training, background, and beliefs.

5. These persons will usually be cooperative and supportive if you establish a good rapport and give them recognition as deserved.

You need to recognize the influences acting upon those other staff members. And you should see yourself as one of those influences. Basically, you ought to consider your ability to interact well with and positively influence the other employees. By concerning yourself with your behaviors and how they influence others, you should be able to make the best of most interactions.

Let us consider some examples. A custodian says to you, "It's really a warm day." You respond, "So what?" Do you think that custodian will be happy to help you with your broken window? You are walking through the office and a secretary says, "Good morning." You ignore her (as usual). Just try to get her to copy some materials in a hurry! Last week you complained about slow service in the cafetera. Did you wonder why there was no rush by the workers there today to help you find some salt?

Here are a few suggestions for developing positive, professional relationships with the school personnel.

1. *Be friendly*. A few words of hello and a nice wish for a good evening or weekend go a long way.

2. *Listen*. When another employee stops to chat, be polite and listen for a moment. Sure you have loads of work to do but it can wait.

3. *Show respect*. No matter what work the person is doing, remember, that work is needed so the education process can continue. Someone has to change the bulbs, sweep the floor, shelve the books, type the letters, and plan the budget.

4. *Offer help*. If you see another worker struggling with a task, lend a hand. That tiny bit of assistance will be remembered and appreciated for a long time.

5. *Be professional*. No matter what level of training an employee has, he or she will recognize if your behavior is professional and appropriate. If you are observed gossiping, lying, or arguing, others may begin to wonder about you.

6. *Be fair*. Treat everyone in a fair and reasonable manner. Many hellos and a

Christmas gift for one particular secretary certainly will not help your working relationships with the other office staff members.

7. *Be reasonable*. Remember that other workers may be doing their best but, because of circumstances beyond their control, their efforts may not produce desired results. Also keep in mind that they may make mistakes—just like you may.

If you keep these guidelines in mind, you should be better prepared to deal with unexpected events involving other school employees. Next you will have a chance to begin thinking about interactions with your co-workers.

Think About It

Avoiding problems through positive efforts can be much more enjoyable than the handling of problems. Therefore, this section will give you an opportunity to brainstorm ways to improve relationships.

For each employee listed, state three ways you can assist that person. Then state three ways in which that person can help you—the teacher.

Librarian
Help I can give

1. _____

2. _____

3. _____

Help I can get

1. _____

2. _____

3. _____

Secretary
Help I can give

1. _____

2. _____

3. _____

Help I can get

1. _____

2. _____

3. _____

Custodian
Help I can give

1. _____

2. _____

3. _____

Help I can get

1. _____

2. _____

3. _____

Bus Driver
Help I can give

1. _____

2. _____

3. _____

Help I can get

1. _____

2. _____

3. _____

Teacher's Aide
Help I can give

1. _____

2. _____

3. _____

Help I can get

1. _____

2. _____

3. _____

Cafeteria Worker
Help I can give

1. _____

2. _____

3. _____

Help I can get

1. _____

2. _____

3. _____

Simulations

The following simulations have been selected to offer you a sampling of unexpected experiences with other school personnel. Keep in mind that you will be dealing with fellow employees who all make contributions to the education of youngsters.

Tough to Do

Setting:	Your classroom
Time:	After school
Person involved:	Clarence Whitmore (an aide)
Background information:	Because of the size of your program, you have had the opportunity to hire an aide. Your principal allowed you to do the interviewing and hiring as long as you would do the firing if ever necessary. You hired Clarence about two months ago.
Circumstances:	Clarence's work is very poor. He makes many errors and he has difficulty following directions. He has also been late on numerous occasions. Last week you told Clarence that you have been disappointed with his work. He was late again today and he couldn't follow directions with two major tasks. You have decided to fire him.
Simulation:	You begin your talk with, "I think I'm going to have to let you go." Clarence says, "Oh, please don't! My wife is expecting and we need the money."

Reactions

1. Will Clarence's arguments change your mind? _____

_____

_____

_____

2. If you should decide to follow through and fire Clarence, what will you say? _____

_____

_____

_____

3. If you should decide to continue Clarence's employment, what will you say? _____

_____

_____

_____

_____

4. Apparently you thought Clarence would be a good aide. What steps could you have taken to insure his success? _____

_____

_____

_____

Effects   What effects will your actions and responses have upon Clarence? _____

_____

_____

_____

Your principal/school? _____

_____

_____

_____

You? _____

_____

_____

_____

Notes   _____

_____

_____

_____

_____

_____

_____

_____

_____

_____

Simulation 6.2 **A New Assignment**

Setting: Your principal's office

Time: During your free period

Person involved: Miss Worthington (your principal)

Background information: You have been teaching at your school for a few years. Miss Worthington is new this year. You are very satisfied with your teaching assignments and expect that they will remain fairly constant over the next few years.

Circumstances: Miss Worthington has asked you to come to her office to discuss your teaching assignment for next year.

Simulation: Miss Worthington tells you that your assignment for next year will include a period of career awareness for handicapped learners. You don't feel qualified to take that teaching assignment and you simply don't want to do it.

Reactions

1. What objectives do you have other than not accepting this new assignment? _____

_____

_____

_____

2. How will you accomplish those objectives? _____

_____

_____

_____

3. What will you say to Miss Worthington? _____

_____

_____

_____

4. Consider the new assignment. What are its positive aspects?

_____

_____

_____

5. What are its negative aspects? _____

_____

_____

_____

Effects   What effects will your actions and responses have upon Miss
Worthington? _____

_____

_____

_____

You? _____

_____

_____

_____

Notes   _____

_____

_____

_____

_____

_____

_____

_____

_____

_____

_____

Simulation 6.3 **Lounge Talk**

Setting:	The teachers' lounge
Time:	During lunch period
Persons involved:	Doug, Harry, and Melissa (all teachers in your school)
Background information:	You have talked briefly with Doug before and he has seemed like a nice person. You have only met Harry and Melissa once before as they are new to your school this year. Sam Goldstein is one of your students. You know that Sam's father has been arrested and Sam has told you some of the details.
Circumstances:	You just got a cup of coffee and Doug asks you to join the three of them. You welcome the opportunity to get to know Harry and Melissa better so you join them. The conversation immediately turns to Mr. Goldstein's arrest.
Simulation:	Harry and Melissa start talking about Mr. Goldstein's arrest. It becomes apparent to you that they have some incorrect information. When you begin to correct them, they start pushing you for details. They also start gossiping about some of Mr. Goldstein's rather inappropriate dealings in town and about his having a girlfriend whom his wife doesn't know about.

Reactions

1. What are your objectives? _____

_____

_____

_____

2. What are your alternatives? _____

_____

_____

_____

3. Assuming that you decide to remain seated with the three teachers, what will you say? _____

_____

_____

_____

4. Should this conversation be reported to your principal? Why?

_____

_____

_____

Effects What effects will your actions and responses have upon the three

teachers? _____

_____

_____

_____

Sam and Mr. Goldstein? _____

_____

_____

_____

Your principal/school? _____

_____

_____

_____

You? _____

_____

_____

_____

Notes _____

_____

_____

_____

_____

_____

_____

_____

_____

_____

Simulation 6.4 **Volunteer or Snoop?**

Setting: Your classroom

Time: Between classes

Person involved: Mrs. Sylvia Redding (a school volunteer)

Background information: Jonathan Redding is a student in one of your classes. His mother, Sylvia Redding, is a volunteer in the school library.

Circumstances: Sylvia has been very pleasant to you since she began working in the school. Lately, however, she has been dropping by to see you at least three times per week. She always asks how Jonathan is doing. Twice last week and again this morning Sylvia stopped by while Jonathan was in class, and he looked quite uncomfortable during her visits.

Simulation: You have decided that you must put a stop to Sylvia's visits. They are time consuming for you and difficult for Jonathan. Sylvia just walked up and asked, "How did Jonathan do this afternoon?" You don't answer the question—you begin to tell Mrs. Redding what you are thinking.

Reactions

1. What will you say? _____

_____

_____

_____

2. Will you report the matter to your school's volunteer coordinator? Why? _____

_____

_____

_____

_____

3. To your principal? Why? _____

_____

_____

_____

_____

4. If Mrs. Redding gets insulted by your insinuations and threat-ens to complain to the principal, what will you say? _____

_____

_____

_____

5. What other alternatives, other than confronting Mrs. Redding, did you have? _____

_____

_____

_____

Effects What effects will your actions and responses have upon Mrs. Redding? _____

_____

_____

Jonathan? _____

_____

_____

Your principal/school? _____

_____

_____

You? _____

_____

_____

Notes _____

_____

_____

_____

_____

_____

_____

Simulation 6.5 **You Call This an Evaluation?**

Setting:	Your classroom
Time:	During one of your classes
Person involved:	Mr. McAdams (your assistant principal)
Background information:	Mr. McAdams has responsibility for completing the annual teacher evaluations in your school. To do this he usually has visited in each teacher's class for about ten minutes, made some notes, and left. You heard a rumor, however, that the principal recently told Mr. McAdams to do a more thorough job. You also heard that Mr. McAdams now is being very demanding and somewhat rude during his visits.
Circumstances:	You heard from one of the school secretaries that Mr. McAdams will be visiting your class today. You have an excellent lesson planned so you are not worried. However, you are determined not to tolerate any of his demanding or rude behavior.
Simulation:	Mr. McAdams walks right into your room during class. He wanders around your room, looks on the bookshelves, looks at your bulletin board, and looks at what you have on your desk. He interrupts and asks to see your lesson plan. Your whispered reply is, "I'm sorry but I don't have one for this lesson." Meanwhile your students are being very distracted from the lesson, but you continue teaching. Then Mr. McAdams interrupts and says, "A better way to teach that would be to . . ." You decide you've had enough and say, "I'd like to speak to you outside the room for a moment."

Reactions

1. What are your objectives? _____

_____

_____

_____

_____

2. What will you say to Mr. McAdams? _____

_____

_____

_____

_____

3. If you get Mr. McAdams angry, your evaluation might suffer. Then what would you do? _____

_____

_____

_____

4. How could you have avoided this problem? _____

_____

_____

_____

5. What can you and your colleagues do about this situation?

_____

_____

_____

Effects   What effects will your actions and responses have upon Mr. McAdams? _____

_____

_____

Your principal/school? _____

_____

_____

Your students? _____

_____

You? _____

_____

_____

Notes   _____

_____

_____

_____

_____

Simulation 6.6 **A Suffering Sub**

Setting:	The hallway outside your classroom
Time:	Late in the morning during one of your classes
Person involved:	Bonita Mendoza (a substitute teacher)
Background information:	Ms. Mendoza is a substitute teacher in the classroom next to yours. When you saw her there this morning, you stopped and said hello. You also offered assistance if needed.
Circumstances:	A few times during the early morning you heard her slam a book on the desk and yell at the students.
Simulation:	There's a soft knock on your door. When you answer the door you see that it is Ms. Mendoza. She says, "I just can't take it anymore. I won't go back in that room—I quit." And she starts crying and sobbing.

Reactions

1. What will you say to Ms. Mendoza? _____

_____

_____

_____

2. Consider the supervision of your students and Ms. Mendoza's students. What will you do? _____

_____

_____

_____

_____

3. Ms. Mendoza could indicate that she would go back if you talked to the students. Would you? If yes, what would you say to the students? If no, what reason would you give to her?

_____

_____

_____

_____

_____

Effects What effects will your actions and responses have upon Ms. Mendoza? _____

_____

_____

_____

Ms. Mendoza's students? _____

_____

_____

_____

Your principal/school? _____

_____

_____

_____

You? _____

_____

_____

_____

Notes _____

_____

_____

_____

_____

_____

_____

_____

_____

_____

Simulation 6.7 **Straight or on the Rocks?**

Setting:	Carl Brandon's classroom
Time:	During lunch period
Person involved:	Carl Brandon (a teacher in your school)
Background information:	You've become somewhat friendly with Carl, a new teacher. You've found him to be pleasant and you assume that he is a good teacher.
Circumstances:	You just found out some good news and you decided to share it with Carl. When you arrive at his room, you see Carl seated at his desk with his back to the door. You impulsively sneak up on him—just for fun.
Simulation:	When you say, "Surprise!" Carl jumps, spills his drink, drops a flask into his briefcase, and turns to you with anger on his face. You smell the liquor and realize that he has been drinking. Carl says (with a slight slur in his speech), "Don't you dare tell anyone about this!"

Reactions

1. What will you say to Carl? _____
_____
_____

2. Will you tell anyone? If so, whom, and what will you say? If no, why? _____
_____
_____

3. Do you regret sneaking up on Carl? Discuss your thoughts.

_____

_____

_____

4. Do you think that Carl Brandon should be allowed to continue as a teacher? Discuss your thoughts. _____

_____

_____

_____

Effects   What effects will your actions and responses have upon Carl?

_____

_____

_____

Your principal/school? _____

_____

_____

_____

You? _____

_____

_____

_____

Notes _____

_____

_____

_____

_____

_____

_____

_____

_____

Simulation 6.8 **Share the Burden**

Setting: Your classroom

Time: During a free period

Person involved: Sally Morgan (a teacher whose classroom is next door to yours)

Background information: You and Sally are team teaching two classes. The original idea was that you would both share the teaching and other duties. This plan had your principal's approval.

Circumstances: Sally simply is not, in your opinion, doing her share. When she teaches, she does so poorly. She is never prepared. And she seems to forget to do things like grading papers, keeping attendance records, and collecting homework. You know you don't want to continue this team teaching arrangement.

Simulation: Sally tells you that she is enjoying team teaching with you. She wants to know if you are willing to do it again next semester.

Reactions

1. What are your objectives? _____

_____

_____

_____

2. How will you respond to Sally's question? _____

_____

_____

_____

3. If your principal were to ask you how the team teaching was working out, what would you say? _____

_____

_____

_____

Effects What effects will your actions and responses have upon Sally Morgan? _____

_____

_____

Your principal/school? _____

_____

_____

_____

The students? _____

_____

_____

_____

You? _____

_____

_____

_____

Notes _____

_____

_____

_____

_____

_____

_____

_____

_____

Good-bye Office Help

Setting:	The school office
Time:	Early morning, before school
Persons involved:	Don Vincente (one of the school's secretaries) and Phil Abrams (the assistant principal)
Background information:	The school secretaries are supposed to do typing for teachers on an "order received" basis. You are on a curriculum committee for your school district, and you have been having a great deal of typing done lately for that committee.
Circumstances:	The curriculum committee meeting scheduled for next week has been suddenly changed to tomorrow. You need to have a report typed today so that it can be copied and be ready for distribution at the meeting.
Simulation:	You walk over to Don's desk and politely ask that he type your work today. He seems upset and says, "You know, you get more typing done than any of the other teachers. And now you want immediate service. Who do you think I am—your private secretary?" As Don is speaking Mr. Abrams walks over, looks at you, and says, "What's going on?"

Reactions

1. How will you answer Mr. Abram's question? _____

_____

_____

_____

2. What can you do to improve your working relationship with Don? _____

_____

_____

_____

3. What can you do to avoid problems like this in the future?

_____

_____

_____

Effects   What effects will your actions and responses have upon Don
Vincente? _____

_____

_____

_____

Phil Abrams? _____

_____

_____

_____

You? _____

_____

_____

_____

Notes   _____

_____

_____

_____

_____

_____

_____

_____

_____

_____

Simulation 6.10 **The Union**

Setting:	Your school auditorium
Time:	During a teachers' union meeting
Persons involved:	Union leaders and teachers
Background information:	For the past two years the teachers in your school district have been represented by the teachers' union. You have been quite involved. Teachers in your school see you as a leader.
Circumstances:	Negotiations for a new contract with your school district have been going poorly. You are concerned because you are afraid of a strike (you need a steady income). However, you feel that the school district has not made an acceptable offer yet.
Simulation:	The chairperson of the union meeting has just announced, "We need to vote on whether to accept the contract offer or strike. But first let's hear from some of you." After two other teachers express their views, he turns to you and says, "You're seen as a leader in your school. What would you suggest we do?"

Reactions

1. What do you know about teachers' unions? _____

_____

_____

_____

2. How would you vote? Why? _____

_____

_____

3. What would you say to your fellow teachers? _____

_____

_____

_____

Effects What effects will your actions and reactions have upon the

union? _____

_____

_____

_____

The other teachers? _____

_____

_____

_____

Your principal/school? _____

_____

_____

_____

You? _____

_____

_____

_____

Notes _____

_____

_____

_____

_____

_____

_____

_____

_____

_____

_____

Simulation 6.11 **A Dirty Room**

Setting:	The hallway outside your classroom
Time:	Between classes
Person involved:	Mr. Headley (a school custodian)
Background information:	Mr. Headley has been a custodian in your school district for more than thirty years. He has always been a very pleasant person.
Circumstances:	One day, about two weeks ago, you found that your classroom had not been cleaned. You didn't say anything. Then last week the same thing happened, so you mentioned it to Mr. Headley. He apologized and immediately cleaned your room. This week your room was missed twice. You mentioned this to a few other teachers and found that they have all been having a similar problem. So you went to your principal and reported the situation.
Simulation:	Mr. Headley has just noticed you in the hall. He walks over and says, "You know you got me in lots of trouble. If you had a complaint, you should have told me. Thanks loads."

Reactions

1. Why do you think Mr. Headley made those statements to you?

_____

_____

2. Do you think a complaint to the principal was appropriate?

_____

_____

_____

3. Apparently the principal indicated to Mr. Headley that you made the complaint. In your opinion was that appropriate? Why?

_____

_____

_____

4. What will you say to Mr. Headley? _____

_____

_____

Effects   What effects will your actions and responses have upon Mr. Headley? _____

_____

_____

_____

Your principal/school? _____

_____

_____

_____

You? _____

_____

_____

_____

Notes   _____

_____

_____

_____

_____

_____

_____

_____

_____

_____

_____

Someone Made a Mistake

Setting: Your principal's office

Time: During the school day

Person involved: Dr. Harrison (the principal)

Background information: Two weeks ago Dr. Harrison sent a memo to all the teachers in your school regarding assignments for next year. You were very upset when you saw that Dr. Harrison intended to change your room. You didn't discuss the issue with her.

Circumstances: Two days after getting Dr. Harrison's memo, you saw your school district subject coordinator. You mentioned to her how upset you were with the impending room change. She indicated that she would talk to Dr. Harrison for you.

Simulation: You have just been called to the office. Dr. Harrison thanks you for coming by her office on such short notice. Then she says, "I am extremely upset that you would try to go over my head about a room change. I'm insulted that you didn't have the decency to talk to me. I'm in charge of this building, not your subject coordinator. Plus, that was a typographical error on the memo. I hadn't intended to change your room anyway."

Reactions

1. What are your objectives? _____

_____

_____

2. What will you say? _____

_____

_____

3. Did you make any errors? What, if any? _____

_____

_____

_____

4. Did your subject coordinator make any errors? What, if any?

_____

_____

_____

5. If you were the principal, how would you have reacted?

_____

_____

_____

Effects   What effects will your actions and responses have upon Dr.
Harrison? _____

_____

_____

_____

Your subject coordinator? _____

_____

_____

_____

You? _____

_____

_____

_____

Notes   _____

_____

_____

_____

_____

_____

_____

_____

_____

The Rest of the Staff

Were you surprised by this chapter? We often forget the interpersonal problems that may exist where we work. In some professions, problems with co-workers are not critical. In teaching, however, it is very important for everyone to work together.

Be sure to realize that all school employees, whether doing direct pupil services or providing support services, have a common goal. That goal is the providing of an excellent education for all students.

It's good to keep in mind that you have a great deal of influence on your relationships with fellow employees. When you treat someone honestly, that person will usually deal honestly with you. When you help someone, that person will usually help you. When you try to communicate, you open an avenue for the other person to communicate with you.

Most problems that teachers face in relating to other staff members can be avoided or their impact reduced greatly. Simply by carefully, logically, and thoughtfully working with others, unexpected events with staff members at your school should be pleasant ones.

Chapter 7

Your Personal Life

Teachers are community role models and public employees. They are therefore often viewed, discussed, praised, and criticized by students, parents, and the community.

What teachers do privately is essentially their business. But as soon as parts of teachers' behaviors are observed or rumored, those behaviors become a reflection on the teacher and the entire school system.

Most unexpected events regarding teachers' personal lives can be avoided. By using logic and common sense, teachers usually can tactfully and quickly handle the events that do occur.

This chapter presents a number of real-life events. Remember, they have happened to other teachers—and they can happen to you.

Factors to Consider

There are generally five categories into which most unexpected events that affect teachers' personal lives fall. They are false accusations, damaging information, student involvement, personal infringement, and different beliefs. Each of these areas deserves attention before you respond to the exercises in preparation for the simulations.

1. You may be faced with the problem of a *false accusation* that would potentially damage your reputation or credibility. For instance, someone may accuse you of having a police record for robbery. If this should occur, you may choose to ignore the incorrect information as long as you feel that it is not particularly damaging. Your reputation and refusal to respond to a false accusation may actually be the best method for handling the situation.

Another tactic would be to inform your principal so that he or she has the correct information. You might also correct the information with other persons, such as with teachers, parents, or students, or by going directly to the source (if known) of the false accusation.

2. There may be *damaging information* about you or your background that you feel may be harmful to your reputation or credibility as a teacher. For instance, you may not want others to know if you had a drinking problem when you were in high school. Or you may feel that it would be inappropriate for others to know of your dating behaviors.

Although these facts would not stop you from being an excellent teacher, you may wish to conceal such information. Therefore, you would need to practice information control and think carefully about divulging your personal secrets.

3. Students often develop crushes on their teachers. This type of situation is found with pupils at every age level. We often think that this is "cute" at the younger ages, but *all* teachers must exercise caution in this area. Overt acts of friendliness may be misconstrued by onlookers or may be misunderstood by the involved students.

The best defense against the problem of *student involvement* is to practice behavior control. Think about how your actions will be perceived before you act. Also remember that any involvement with students outside appropriate school activities may be frowned upon, and serious involvements may lead to immediate dismissal. It is wise to not be alone with a student, because a situation could develop in which your best intentions are misunderstood.

4. As a teacher you may be faced with the problem of *personal infringement.* You are hired to teach. You may also be expected to conduct many other educational activities, such as patrolling hallways,

supervising social programs, meeting with parents, and coaching athletics. When your school, your students, or your students' parents pressure you to do more than what you have been hired to do and desire to do, then you are faced with a problem.

When this situation occurs, you will need to decide how and with what pressure to resist. It may be sufficient to simply say no. You may need to elicit assistance from your teachers' union or association or from your principal. Or you may need to carefully and directly explain to the persons who are infringing why you are unable or unwilling to fulfill their requests.

5. The last category of events that affects teachers' personal lives is *different beliefs.* For instance, you may have certain preferences that differ from your school's policies regarding curriculum content. Or you may have different expectations in such areas as behavior control, emphasis on athletics, health examinations, and school budget.

Each time you disagree with your school's policies and practices, you need to make a decision. Will you accept the school's policy? Reject the policy and, therefore, be in violation of it? Study the policy and perhaps reconsider your position? Or will you constructively work toward modifying the policy?

Different circumstances and your level of disagreement will help you decide what to do. Be sure to consider these four possibilities before making your decision: Be open-minded, study the policy carefully, review your position, and consider the ramifications of your action or inaction.

Think About It

Before you begin the pre-simulation exercises, brainstorm with your peers for possible responses to the following three questions. Then write your reactions in the provided spaces. These questions should help you begin your consideration of unexpected events regarding teaching and your personal life.

Consider that you are a school principal for these questions:

1. One of your students informed you that he or she was kissed by one of the teachers. What would you do? _____

_____

_____

_____

2. You have asked one of your teachers to accompany a school group on a weekend-long field trip. The teacher has politely refused due to "personal commitments." The same teacher refused to take a similar assignment before. What action will you

take? _____

_____

_____

_____

3. An active member of your school's parent organization complained to you that he saw one of your teachers leaving a local nightclub and that the teacher appeared to be drunk. What will you say to the parent?

_____

_____

_____

To the teacher? _____

_____

_____

_____

Simulations

Now it is time to consider and complete the pre-simulation exercises. When you are finished, you should be ready to participate in the role-play activities.

Every one of these events, and many more like them, have happened to teachers. Consider them carefully so that you will be better prepared should one of these events confront you.

Simulation 7.1 **No Kiss and Tell**

Setting:	Your classroom
Time:	During your lunch break
Persons involved:	Two of your students, Steve and Theresa
Background information:	Steve, Theresa, and you have an excellent relationship. They are pleasant, intelligent students. They know you better than most pupils. You have been tutoring Sandy, one of your other students, after school for the past two weeks.
Circumstances:	During your tutoring sessions, you have noticed that Sandy has been looking at you with "a certain glow." You decided to ignore the behavior, hoping it would go away.
Simulation:	Steve and Theresa come to see you. They are very serious and tell you that they overheard Sandy telling some friends about how well you kiss. One of Sandy's friends remarked about seeing the two of you kissing. You tell Steve and Theresa that the story is not true, but they don't believe you.

Reactions 1. What are you going to say to Steve and Theresa? _____

_____

_____

_____

2. Will you involve your principal? If so, what will you say? If not, why? _____

_____

_____

3. Will you speak to Sandy? If so, what will you say? If not, why?

_____

_____

_____

4. What other actions will you take? Why? _____

_____

_____

_____

5. What errors, if any, did you make that may have caused this problem? _____

_____

_____

_____

Effects   What effects will your actions and responses have upon Sandy?

_____

_____

_____

Steve and Theresa? _____

_____

_____

_____

Other students? _____

_____

_____

_____

Your principal/school? _____

_____

_____

_____

You? _____

_____

_____

_____

Notes   _____

_____

_____

_____

_____

_____

Simulation 7.2 **A Hug Equals Love**

Setting:	Your principal's office
Time:	During the school day
Person involved:	Dr. Hill (the principal)
Background information:	Dr. Hill is a much-respected principal who is known for being demanding but fair. He has always been very pleasant toward you.
Circumstances:	Last week a student, who is the same sex as you, came into your classroom to tell you wonderful news of being selected for a part in the school play. You gave the student a big hug of congratulations.
Simulation:	Dr. Hill asks you to have a seat in his office. He promptly and seriously tells you that Mrs. Perkins, another teacher, observed you hugging a student who is the same sex as you. The description of the student makes you realize that the student was the one you were congratulating. Before you can explain, Dr. Hill requests your immediate resignation because of "unacceptable sexual behavior in the school building."

Reactions

1. How do you feel right now toward Dr. Hill? _____

_____

_____

2. What are you going to say to Dr. Hill? _____

_____

_____

3. What, if anything, will you say to Mrs. Perkins? _____

_____

_____

_____

4. Do you intend to involve the student in your "defense"? If so, how? If not, why? _____

_____

_____

_____

5. Apparently Mrs. Perkins misunderstood what she observed. Would you give a congratulatory hug again, realizing the risk involved? Why? _____

_____

_____

_____

Effects What effects will your actions and responses have upon Dr. Hill?

_____

_____

_____

Mrs. Perkins? _____

_____

_____

_____

The student you hugged? _____

_____

_____

_____

You? _____

_____

_____

_____

Notes _____

_____

_____

_____

_____

_____

_____

_____

_____

Simulation 7.3 **Partly True**

Setting: The teachers' lounge

Time: During lunch period

Person involved: Darin Farnsworth (a fellow teacher and friend)

Background information: You were arrested a few months ago for drunk driving, but the charges were reduced to reckless driving. You are going to driving school as part of your penalty. This was your first traffic violation.

Circumstances: You have not told anyone at school about being arrested.

Simulation: Darin has just sat down next to you. With a serious look on his face he says, "Well I hate to tell you this but everyone is talking about your being a drunk driver. I heard that you've been jailed for drunk driving twice now. Is that true?"

Reactions
1. What will you say to Darin? _____
   _____
   _____

2. Will you say or do anything else about the gossip? What?
   _____
   _____
   _____

3. Will you now tell your principal about the ticket? Why?
   _____
   _____
   _____

4. How do you feel toward Darin? _____
   _____
   _____

5. How do you feel toward the other teachers? _____
   _____
   _____
   _____

Effects   What effects will your actions and responses have upon Darin?

_____

_____

_____

The other teachers? _____

_____

_____

_____

Your principal/school? _____

_____

_____

_____

You? _____

_____

_____

_____

Notes   _____

_____

_____

_____

_____

_____

_____

_____

_____

_____

Simulation 7.4 **Nosy Students**

Setting:	In the school cafeteria
Time:	During the lunch hour
Persons involved:	Six students who are in your classes
Background information:	You have recently begun dating someone. You've been seeing him/her rather frequently. Your date happens to be a person well-known in your community.
Circumstances:	You are walking through the cafeteria. There's a table of six students nearby. The students are sitting around, talking loudly, and laughing. One of the students sees you and calls your name, so you walk over to see what he wants.
Simulation:	You start the conversation with, "Hi everyone! Sounds like you're all enjoying yourselves. What are you all gabbing about?" The response you get is, "You and your new girl (boy) friend! She's (he's) really sexy. Have you been in bed with her (him) yet?" The students continue their laughter and questions.

Reactions 1. What are you going to say to the students about your date?

_____

_____

_____

2. What are you going to say to the students about their behavior? _____

_____

_____

_____

3. Will you take any action against the students due to their behavior? If so, what? If not, why? _____

_____

_____

_____

_____

4. How will this event affect your relationship with your date?

_____

_____

_____

Effects   What effects will your actions and responses have upon the six students? _____

_____

_____

_____

Your principal/school? _____

_____

_____

_____

You? _____

_____

_____

_____

Notes _____

_____

_____

_____

_____

_____

_____

_____

_____

_____

_____

_____

Simulation 7.5 **I Heard You're Cool**

Setting: Your classroom

Time: Between classes

Persons involved: Cheryl Ilnicki and Rita Barsky (two of your students)

Background information: You are good friends with Cheryl's older brother, Stanley. In fact you have been out with Stanley many evenings. You both have done some drinking and have smoked some marijuana together. You've often joked that Cheryl better not find out about your behavior.

Circumstances: You are working at your desk. Rita walks in and you two are alone in the room.

Simulation: Rita says, "I heard you're cool." Your response is, "What does that mean?" She proceeds to tell you that she heard from Cheryl that you smoke pot. Before you have a chance to say anything, Cheryl walks in.

Reactions

1. What will you say to Rita? _____

_____

_____

_____

2. What will you say to Cheryl? _____

_____

_____

_____

3. When you get the chance, what will you say to Stanley?

_____

_____

_____

4. Since the information is true and potentially damaging, what else can you do? _____

_____

_____

5. How can you avoid problems like this in the future?

_____

_____

_____

Effects   What effects will your actions and responses have upon Rita?

_____

_____

_____

Cheryl? _____

_____

_____

_____

Stanley? _____

_____

_____

_____

Your principal/school? _____

_____

_____

_____

You? _____

_____

_____

_____

Notes _____

_____

_____

_____

_____

_____

_____

Fun on the Phone

Setting: Your classroom

Time: During class

Persons involved: T. J. Martinez (one of your students) and the rest of your students

Background information: T. J. has only been in your class for about two weeks. Soon after T. J. arrived, you began getting obscene phone calls during the evening. You quickly hung up on all occasions. You have also advised your principal of the calls. Last night the same caller made very direct comments about wanting to engage in sexual activities with you.

Circumstances: You suspect that T. J. is the caller, so you've decided to bring the subject of the phone calls up in today's class.

Simulation: You tell the class about getting inappropriate calls and that you suspect someone from class is making the calls. Two people tell on T. J. and confirm your suspicions. T. J. begins to cry and states, "But I only did it because I love you." The rest of the students snicker and laugh.

Reactions

1. What will you say to the class? _____

_____

_____

2. What will you say to T. J.? Privately? In front of the class?

_____

_____

_____

3. If some of the students or T. J. call the two persons who told "pets" or "tattletales," what will you say? _____

_____

_____

_____

4. How else could you have handled this problem? _____

_____

_____

Effects   What effects will your actions and responses have upon T. J.?

_____

_____

_____

The other students? _____

_____

_____

_____

Your principal/school? _____

_____

_____

_____

You? _____

_____

_____

_____

Notes   _____

_____

_____

_____

_____

_____

_____

_____

_____

Simulation 7.7 **Young Love**

Setting:	Your house
Time:	One Saturday afternoon
Person involved:	Julie (one of the students from your school)
Background information:	Julie lives only a few blocks from your home. You have often seen Julie, and on occasion you've stopped and talked to this pleasant, attractive student.
Circumstances:	While working in your front yard, you notice Julie walking down the street. You wave and Julie walks over. Julie seems depressed, so you say, "Let's go inside and have a cold drink."
Simulation:	As soon as you get inside, Julie starts telling you that the depression is caused by not being able to tell a secret love about the loving feelings. You suggest that Julie should be honest. So before you realize what's happening, Julie gives you a big kiss and says, "You're the one I love."

Reactions

1. What is your major objective? _____

_____

_____

_____

2. What will you say to Julie? _____

_____

_____

_____

3. Will you have your discussion in your house? Why?

_____

_____

_____

4. Will you tell your principal about this incident? If yes, what will you say? If no, why not? _____

_____

_____

5. Will you talk to Julie's parents about the situation? If yes, what will you say? If no, why not? _____

_____

_____

_____

Effects   What effects will your actions and responses have upon Julie?

_____

_____

_____

Your principal/school? _____

_____

_____

_____

You? _____

_____

_____

_____

Notes   _____

_____

_____

_____

_____

_____

_____

_____

_____

_____

_____

Simulation 7.8 **Parents Put Plenty Pressure**

Setting:	Your home
Time:	Early evening
Person involved:	Mrs. Williams (a member of your school's Parent-Teacher Organization)
Background information:	You have been very active in sponsoring school activities. Last year you were honored by the PTO for your efforts.
Circumstances:	Mrs. Williams, the newly elected chairperson of the PTO, left a note in your mailbox last week. She said that she's "looking forward to your continued assistance this school year." However, you have decided to take some courses and will not have time for the activities you formerly directed.
Simulation:	You receive a telephone call from Mrs. Williams. After an exchange of greetings, she asks you to become involved in a few new PTO-sponsored activities. You politely refuse. Mrs. Williams becomes insulted, takes your "no" personally, and continues to ask, then plead, for your assistance. She just won't take no for an answer.

Reactions

1. What will you say so that Mrs. Williams won't take your "no" personally? _____

_____

_____

_____

2. What will you say to convince a persistent Mrs. Williams that you are not available? _____

_____

_____

_____

3. How can you assist Mrs. Williams without committing yourself to any work? _____

_____

_____

4. Mrs. Williams just doesn't want to give up. How can you end this long conversation politely? _____

_____

_____

_____

Effects What effects will your actions and responses have upon Mrs. Williams? _____

_____

_____

_____

Your principal/school? _____

_____

_____

_____

You? _____

_____

_____

_____

Notes _____

_____

_____

_____

_____

_____

_____

_____

_____

_____

Simulation 7.9 **Give an Inch and . . .**

Setting: Your principal's office

Time: During a free period

Persons involved: Dr. Cunningham (your principal) and Ms. Sharkey (a special education teacher)

Background information: You have always been an energetic teacher who has tried to work well with all students. Last year you agreed to work with a couple of handicapped learners who were mainstreamed into regular classes. You know that a number of other teachers had refused to have handicapped children in their classes. You consider this to be unfair and unprofessional on their part.

Circumstances: Dr. Cunningham asked you to come to her office to discuss your mainstreaming efforts. As you arrive, you notice that Ms. Sharkey has just stepped into the office.

Simulation: After an exchange of greetings, Dr. Cunningham and Ms. Sharkey commend you for your work with handicapped students. Your principal then tells you that she would like you to have more mainstreamed students. Your initial thought is that you are already overworked, and you also think about those teachers who have no handicapped students.

Reactions

1. What are your objectives? _____

_____

_____

_____

2. What will you say to Dr. Cunningham and Ms. Sharkey about already being overworked? _____

_____

_____

_____

3. What will you say about the other teachers? _____

_____

_____

_____

4. If asked for suggestions regarding the other teachers, what will you say? _____

_____

_____

5. If Dr. Cunningham puts pressure on you to accept the additional pupils, what will you say? _____

_____

_____

Effects   What effects will your actions and responses have upon Dr. Cunningham? _____

_____

_____

Ms. Sharkey? _____

_____

_____

The students? _____

_____

_____

The other teachers? _____

_____

_____

You? _____

_____

_____

Notes   _____

_____

_____

_____

_____

_____

Simulation 7.10 I Don't Want to Teach That!

Setting: A teacher workshop

Time: On an inservice training day

Persons involved: Dr. Taylor (your school district's director of curriculum) and other teachers attending the workshop.

Background information: During the past two months Dr. Taylor has circulated a number of new textbooks among some teachers. You have reviewed them carefully in case your input was sought regarding their possible adoption. In fact, that is supposedly one of the items on the agenda for today's workshop.

Circumstances: You are attending the workshop. After a few interesting presentations Dr. Taylor announces that textbook adoption is the next topic.

Simulation: Dr. Taylor announces that he has selected new textbooks for next year. One, which you would be required to use, is a book that you dislike. You state your displeasure and a few of your colleagues whisper their agreement to you. Dr. Taylor states, "The decision has been made, but I would be happy to hear your reasons."

Reactions

1. List some criteria for evaluating a textbook. _____

_____

_____

_____

2. What will you say to Dr. Taylor about the selection process?

_____

_____

_____

3. What will you say to Dr. Taylor about the book? _____

_____

_____

_____

_____

4. Will you challenge your colleagues to give their input? If yes, what will you say? If no, why not? _____

_____

_____

_____

Effects   What effects will your actions and responses have upon Dr. Taylor? _____

_____

_____

_____

The other teachers? _____

_____

_____

_____

Your principal/school? _____

_____

_____

_____

You? _____

_____

_____

_____

Notes   _____

_____

_____

_____

_____

_____

_____

_____

Simulation 7.11 **Budget Woes**

Setting:	A faculty meeting
Time:	After school hours
Persons involved:	Mrs. Von Lehe (your principal) and the rest of the school faculty
Background information:	During the past two months you have had two purchase requests turned down. You had wanted to buy some hand-held calculators and some new workbooks for your classes. You also know, from talking to your school's librarian, that the library's budget request was cut in half by Mrs. Von Lehe.
Circumstances:	After conducting some general school business, Mrs. Von Lehe announced that she ordered three new gym mats and new carpeting for the school's entrance area and her office. Someone else asked how much those cost. Mrs. Von Lehe stated, "Only about $2,000." Another teacher raised his hand and said that he had wanted to buy some supplies for his classes and was turned down. He couldn't understand why Mrs. Von Lehe could go ahead and make these other purchases. Mrs. Von Lehe stated that she must have misplaced that request and that she had received no others so she decided to spend the remaining budget for the year on her two projects.
Simulation:	You notice that the librarian is looking disgusted and that he is raising his hand to speak. Your arm instinctively goes up in the air. Mrs. Von Lehe looks at you and says, "Yes, what is it?"

Reactions

1. What are your objectives? _____

_____

_____

2. What will you say about Mrs. Von Lehe's purchases?

_____

_____

_____

3. What will you say about your requests that were denied?

_____

_____

_____

4. Will you say anything about the cuts in the library budget? If yes, what? If no, why? _____

_____

_____

_____

5. If Mrs. Von Lehe politely thanks you and goes on to other business, what options do you have? _____

_____

_____

_____

Effects   What effects will your actions and responses have upon Mrs. Von Lehe? _____

_____

_____

_____

The other teachers? _____

_____

_____

_____

You? _____

_____

_____

_____

Notes   _____

_____

_____

_____

_____

_____

_____

_____

Simulation 7.12 **Not as Expected**

Setting:	The school conference room
Time:	During a faculty meeting
Persons involved:	Sister Agnes (the principal) and other faculty members
Background information:	You have accepted a teaching position in a parochial school. You understood that you would not need to be involved in any religious activities. That was important to you since your faith is different from the school's.
Circumstances:	Sister Agnes is making a number of announcements to the faculty.
Simulation:	Sister Agnes casually mentions that "all teachers should read Bible passages whenever there is a free moment." You ask, "Is that required?" Her response is, "Certainly—oh, I forgot. Well you can certainly read Bible passages, can't you?" You can't.

Reactions

1. What are your objectives? _____

_____

_____

_____

2. What are your options? _____

_____

_____

_____

_____

3. What will you say? _____

_____

_____

_____

4. How could you have avoided this problem? _____

_____

_____

_____

Effects   What effects will your actions and responses have upon Sister Agnes? _____

_____

_____

_____

The other teachers? _____

_____

_____

_____

You? _____

_____

_____

_____

Notes   _____

_____

_____

_____

_____

_____

_____

_____

_____

Your Personal Life

Yes, all of these events are real. They have happened to teachers like yourself. And many times events such as these have produced hardships, anguish, frustration, and disappointment.

The simulations presented are samples of events from the five categories discussed earlier. By considering problems like these now, you will be able to devise strategies that will help you avoid similar events or at least mitigate their impact.

In all cases, you should attempt to recognize the position and attitudes of others. You should try to predict how your actions and statements will be interpreted. And you should fully consider the immediate and long-term effects of your reactions.

Unlike many unexpected health and safety events, these situations usually don't require split-second decision making. Carefully think about the what, why, when, where, and how of your responses. And be sure to consider the effects of your behaviors on your students and on your teaching career.

Most times, problems affecting teachers' personal lives are handled without any lasting difficulties. With prior thought and role-playing of these situations, you should be better prepared to reduce the impact of similar events when they happen to you.

Chapter 8

For the Student Teacher

This chapter has been designed for those of you who are anticipating an internship or student teaching experience. No doubt you have taken many college courses and have observed and worked with school pupils as part of your training. If you are like many others, you are probably quite excited and, at the same time, somewhat nervous about student teaching.

Student teaching is usually the culmination of your training—an opportunity for you to demonstrate your abilities and prove that you are worthy of being a teacher. You will be observed and judged by your college supervisor, the classroom teacher (often called the supervising or directing teacher), your principal, the other staff members, the parents, and the students.

We are going to assume that you are ready for student teaching. You have worked hard, you have a thorough knowledge of the content you expect to teach, you are able to construct tests, you have evaluation skills, and so forth. Generally you are very well prepared.

By having done the pre-simulation exercises in this book you have readied yourself to handle unexpected events. By participating in role-play activities with your peers you feel somewhat confident in dealing with a variety of occurrences. But are you ready for events unique to student teachers? This chapter will help you prepare.

Factors to Consider

Student teaching is the next best thing to being there. You're in charge—but you're not. You do the planning—but it's checked. You teach—but you're being evaluated. You handle the unexpected—but you know the teacher will help if needed. Actually you have a backup person for everything you do as a teacher. Therefore this next section will offer you ten guidelines for the things you do as a student teacher—when a backup is not present.

1. *Don't be afraid to ask.* When something is occurring that you don't understand, ask the directing teacher or college supervisor. This pertains to everything— testing, teaching, handling of unexpected events, curriculum, statements, directions—everything.

2. *Be prepared.* You will need to put a great deal of energy into all of your duties. If you are not ready to return materials, to teach a lesson, or to do any of the many tasks of teaching when they are expected, then you will have difficulties.

3. *Be organized.* Keep notes on everything you need to do. Keep a calendar so you will know when you are expected somewhere. These hints will help you do what you are supposed to do when expected.

4. *Get to know everyone.* Be friendly with all of the school's staff members. Meet the secretaries, custodians, volunteers—everyone who is part of your school's team. If you know them, you will be able to call upon them when needed.

5. *Be honest.* Don't be afraid to admit your limitations and errors to your directing teacher and to your students. They are not looking for a perfect superhuman. Both the students and directing teacher know you are a real person.

6. *Follow directions.* Be sure to remember that you are a guest in the directing teacher's classroom. You need to do your work that teacher's way unless you are given latitude to follow your own instincts and to use ideas you have been taught. Be sure to ask if you would like to try something new. The directing teacher will probably be very supportive.

7. *Ask for critique.* Some directing teachers are uncomfortable giving criticism. However, you should want constructive criticism so that you can improve as a teacher. If critique is not offered, ask for it.

8. *Be professional.* Dress correctly. Act appropriately. Maintain confidentiality. Behave like a teacher. Remember you are being evaluated in everything you do and say.

9. *Think before you act.* Be sure to consider the consequences of everything you do. Think of how your behaviors will be perceived by others.

10. *Maintain control.* Remember that you are at the school to teach, not to be friends with the students.

Think About It

Here is your opportunity to take a good look at yourself. In the space below list all of the things a teacher has to be able to do.

Now go back through the list and circle those tasks you feel confident to handle. Then list in the space below those tasks that you did not circle but that you feel are critically needed by teachers.

Is the above space empty? If not, you know what you must practice or study before you student teach. Confidence in your abilities will help you in the simulations that follow and when you are a teacher.

Simulations

The following simulations are unique to persons in the position of student teacher. Keep in mind that these events may occur *in addition to* all of the others in the earlier chapters of the book.

Bored to Death

Setting:	Your classroom
Time:	After school
Person involved:	Mrs. Clarkson (your directing teacher)
Background information:	You have been a student teacher for almost two weeks. On your first day Mrs. Clarkson said, "Just sit in the back and observe. I'll get you started when you're ready."
Circumstances:	You are absolutely bored. You've been sitting and watching for days and you are anxious to do some teaching. Mrs. Clarkson says she would like to talk to you today after school.
Simulation:	At the after school conference Mrs. Clarkson asks you if you have any questions about her teaching style or about the students. After she answers these questions, she says, "Well maybe we'll get you started in another week or two." You decide you can't wait any longer.

Reactions

1. What will you say? _____

_____

_____

_____

2. Will you discuss the problem with your college supervisor?

_____

_____

_____

3. What will you do if Mrs. Clarkson says, "No, I think you need to observe for a while longer?" _____

_____

_____

Effects What effects will your actions and responses have upon Mrs. Clarkson? _____

_____

_____

Your college supervisor? _____

_____

_____

_____

You? _____

_____

_____

_____

Notes _____

_____

_____

_____

_____

_____

_____

_____

_____

_____

_____

Substitute Time

Setting:	Your classroom
Time:	Monday morning, before school
Person involved:	Mr. Myerowitz (the school principal)
Background information:	Your college supervisor had indicated to your seminar that student teachers should not be used as substitute teachers for liability reasons.
Circumstances:	You are in your seventh week as a student teacher. All of your evaluations have been excellent and you are feeling quite confident. Your directing teacher, Mr. Sims, has essentially left you alone with his classes for three days while he worked on a curriculum project in the office. All three days went very smoothly.
Simulation:	Mr. Myerowitz has stopped in to see you. He says, "I just got a call from Mr. Sims. He is ill and can't make it in today. He indicated that you were planning to teach the entire day. So, since you've been doing so well, I've decided not to hire a substitute. I'm sure you'll be fine, but if you have any problems, just call me in my office."

Reactions

1. How do you feel? Pleased? Used? Confused? Explain.

_____

_____

_____

2. What will you say to Mr. Myerowitz? _____

_____

_____

_____

3. What will you tell your college supervisor? _____

_____

_____

_____

_____

Effects   What effects will your actions and responses have upon Mr. Myerowitz? _____

_____

_____

_____

Mr. Sims? _____

_____

_____

_____

Your college supervisor? _____

_____

_____

_____

You? _____

_____

_____

_____

Notes   _____

_____

_____

_____

_____

_____

_____

_____

_____

_____

Simulation 8.3 **They're Testing You**

Setting: Your classroom

Time: During your third period class

Persons involved: Miss Donohoe (your directing teacher) and your students

Background information: You have been a student teacher in Miss Donohoe's class for four weeks now. She has steadily given you added responsibilities. Last week you began teaching complete lessons on your own. After those lessons Miss Donohoe has given you suggestions. She has been pleased that you haven't had any behavior problems.

Circumstances: Earlier today Miss Donohoe said, "This morning, during third period, you are going to be on your own. I'm sure you'll be OK, but if you need me, I'll be in the teachers' lounge."

Simulation: Third period has just begun. Although you are a bit concerned about being alone for the first time, everything starts out smoothly. One student raises her hand and asks, "Where's Miss Donohoe?" You respond, "She won't be here this period." That must have been a signal because during the next few minutes talking, throwing of paper, and out-of-seat behavior starts and is more than you have seen in the past four weeks put together. You know that you need to stop this bad behavior.

Reactions

1. What could you have said to the class to have prevented the problem? _____

_____

_____

2. Why do you think the bad behavior started? _____

_____

_____

_____

3. What will you say or do to stop the bad behavior? _____

_____

_____

_____

4. What will you tell Miss Donohoe when she returns? _____

_____

_____

_____

Effects What effects will your actions and responses have upon Miss Donohoe? _____

_____

_____

_____

Your students? _____

_____

_____

_____

Your college supervisor? _____

_____

_____

_____

You? _____

_____

_____

_____

Notes _____

_____

_____

_____

_____

_____

_____

_____

Simulation 8.4 **No News Is Good News?**

Setting:	Your classroom
Time:	Friday—at the end of the school day
Person involved:	Mr. Sherry (your directing teacher)
Background information:	Mr. Sherry is very competent and you are happy to have him as your directing teacher. He has been allowing you to try the materials and methods you have learned in your college classes.
Circumstances:	You are just completing your fifth week of student teaching. You've been very pleased since each week, during your Friday afternoon conference, Mr. Sherry has been telling you that he is very satisfied with your work. But he has never given you any direction or criticism, and you know you have room for improvement. You've discussed the situation with your college supervisor, and she has suggested that you ask for, and if necessary insist upon, more feedback.
Simulation:	You and Mr. Sherry just sat down for your regular Friday afternoon conference. He says, "Well, you're continuing to do very well. Keep up the good work." You say, "Well, I'm pleased but I'd really appreciate any suggestions you may have." He says, "Oh don't worry, everything is fine." That doesn't satisfy you.

Reactions

1. Why should you want more feedback than what Mr. Sherry is offering? _____

_____

_____

2. What can you say to him so that he is encouraged to give more feedback? _____

_____

_____

3. Should you ask your college supervisor to discuss the lack of critique with Mr. Sherry? Why? _____

_____

_____

_____

Effects   What effects will your actions and responses have upon Mr. Sherry? _____

_____

_____

Your college supervisor? _____

_____

_____

_____

You? _____

_____

_____

_____

Notes   _____

_____

_____

_____

_____

_____

_____

_____

_____

_____

_____

Simulation 8.5 **Sure I Can**

Setting: Your classroom

Time: During a class period

Persons involved: Ms. Smith (your directing teacher) and your class

Background information: You're in your first week of student teaching. Ms. Smith has asked you to tell some things about yourself to your students so that they would get to know you better.

Circumstances: You are speaking to the class and you tell them about being a college student. You also tell them about having been a scout when you were younger. Some students ask questions about scouting, so you tell them how you became very skilled in things like canoeing, fire building, and rope tying. Then you tell the class that you still can do everything you learned in scouting.

Simulation: One student asks if you would demonstrate some rope tying. You respond (while thinking that you never could tie knots well), "Oh no, I'm sorry but there won't be time for that." But Ms. Smith interrupts and says, "Oh, that's OK, we can take some time for that. I'd like to see the different ways to tie knots, also. Here's some rope."

Reactions

1. What are you going to say to the class? _____

_____

_____

_____

2. What will you say to Ms. Smith? _____

_____

_____

_____

3. How could you have avoided this problem? _____

_____

_____

_____

_____

Effects   What effects will your actions and responses have upon Ms. Smith? _____

_____

_____

_____

Your students? _____

_____

_____

Your college supervisor? _____

_____

_____

You? _____

_____

_____

Notes   _____

_____

_____

_____

_____

_____

_____

_____

_____

Simulation 8.6 **Why This Time?**

Setting: Your classroom

Time: During a class period

Persons involved: Mrs. Walsh (your college supervisor) and Mr. Schmid (your directing teacher)

Background information: You have been teaching the fourth period class for six days now. Every lesson you presented went very well. Yesterday's fourth period class was the best yet. Today, at the end of third period, Mrs. Walsh arrived. You naturally got a bit nervous since you knew she would be evaluating you. You didn't expect her today but consoled yourself by thinking that fourth period is your best.

Circumstances: Well, fourth period today was your worst. The students wouldn't pay attention, there was a fight between two students, your students couldn't understand the activity you had planned, and the overhead projector bulb burned out just when you needed it. When the bell rang you were exhausted, irritated, and embarrassed.

Simulation: As the students leave, Mrs. Walsh asks you to join her and Mr. Schmid in the back of the room. You sit down with them. Mrs. Walsh starts the discussion with, "Well, why don't you talk about what just went on."

Reactions 1. What are your objectives? _____

_____

_____

_____

2. What will you say about this particular period? _____

_____

_____

_____

3. Would you want Mr. Schmid to come to your defense? Why?

_____

_____

_____

4. Do you expect that this observation will greatly influence your student teaching grade? Why? _____

_____

_____

_____

Effects What effects will your actions and responses have upon Mrs. Walsh? _____

_____

_____

_____

Mr. Schmid? _____

_____

_____

_____

You? _____

_____

_____

_____

Notes _____

_____

_____

_____

_____

_____

_____

_____

_____

_____

_____

_____

Simulation 8.7 **Not the Real Thing**

Setting:	The school office
Time:	After school
Person involved:	Mrs. Bloom (mother of Vikki Bloom, one of your students)
Background information:	For the past two weeks your directing teacher has given you a great deal of responsibility for planning and teaching. She has told you that she wants you to feel as though the class is really yours.
Circumstances:	Vikki has not done her homework for your class for the past three days. You suggested to your directing teacher that perhaps you should call Mrs. Bloom and discuss the problem. Your directing teacher agreed.
Simulation:	When you reach Mrs. Bloom by phone, you identify yourself and say, "The reason I'm calling is because Vikki hasn't been doing her homework." Mrs. Bloom says, "Wait a second. Aren't you the student teacher?" You say, "Yes, but I have been . . ." Mrs. Bloom interrupts and says, "Listen, I don't want to talk to a student teacher. If there's a problem, I want to talk to the real teacher!"

Reactions

1. What are your objectives? _____

_____

_____

2. What are your options? _____

_____

_____

3. What will you say to Mrs. Bloom? _____

_____

_____

_____

4. What will you say to your directing teacher? _____

_____

_____

_____

Effects   What effects will your actions and responses have upon Mrs. Bloom? _____

_____

_____

_____

Your directing teacher? _____

_____

_____

_____

You? _____

_____

_____

_____

Notes   _____

_____

_____

_____

_____

_____

_____

_____

_____

_____

Simulation 8.8 **Work! Work! Work!**

Setting: Your college supervisor's office

Time: One afternoon after school during your third week of student teaching

Person involved: Dr. Burke (your college supervisor)

Background information: You have always been a very successful college student. You studied hard right before your tests and in that way you earned excellent grades. You have also been very involved with college activities and you have maintained part-time employment.

Circumstances: While student teaching you have cut down your part-time employment to fifteen hours per week. You have dropped some of your college activities, but still you have been finding it difficult to do everything. Recently you have been late with grading papers and negligent about planning lessons. Although you thought you were working very hard on student teaching, your directing teacher told you that she was not satisfied with your work.

Simulation: Dr. Burke called this morning and asked you to come by his office this afternoon. After greeting you he says, "Do you realize that your directing teacher is not satisfied with your student teaching performance?" You respond, "Yes, but I have been working very hard." Dr. Burke says, "But I don't think it's been hard enough. Perhaps you should drop out for the rest of this term and try again later—when student teaching can be your number one priority."

Reactions

1. Since you don't want to drop out, what can you say?

_____

_____

_____

2. What can you do to improve your performance? _____

_____

_____

3. What will you say to your directing teacher? _____

_____

_____

4. Must student teaching be your number one priority? Why?

_____

_____

_____

Effects   What effects will your actions and responses have upon Dr. Burke? _____

_____

_____

_____

Your directing teacher? _____

_____

_____

_____

You? _____

_____

_____

_____

Notes   _____

_____

_____

_____

_____

_____

_____

_____

_____

_____

_____

Simulation 8.9 **Second-Rate Citizen**

Setting:	The principal's conference room
Time:	One afternoon after school during the fourth week of student teaching
Persons involved:	Mrs. Baxter (your school principal) and three other student teachers
Background information:	You and the three other student teachers in the school have been eating lunch every day in the teachers' lounge. The lounge is quite small, but everyone has squeezed a bit so that all could be accommodated.
Circumstances:	Yesterday, Mr. Crabtree, one of the teachers, couldn't find a seat at a table in the teachers' lounge. So he ate his lunch while sitting at a small desk. You overheard him complaining to a couple of teachers that because of the *%@$!*&¢ student teachers he couldn't even have a pleasant lunch period.
Simulation:	After general greetings Mrs. Baxter indicates that someone has complained that the teachers' lounge is too small to accommodate the student teachers during lunch. She says, "I hate to have to ask you to stay out. Do you have any ideas?" You decide to offer your suggestions.

Reactions

1. What are the options? _____

_____

_____

_____

2. Which will you support? Why? _____

_____

_____

_____

3. What will you say to Mrs. Baxter? _____

_____

_____

_____

_____

4. Next time you see Mr. Crabtree will you discuss the situation with him? Why? _____

_____

_____

_____

Effects   What effects will your actions and responses have upon Mrs. Baxter? _____

_____

_____

_____

The teachers? _____

_____

_____

Mr. Crabtree? _____

_____

_____

Notes   _____

_____

_____

_____

_____

_____

_____

_____

_____

_____

Simulation 8.10 **Sick in Bed**

Setting:	Your bedroom
Time:	Approximately 7:30 A.M. on a school day
Person involved:	Mr. Stevenson (your directing teacher)
Background information:	During a pre-student teaching seminar your college supervisor announced that if you are ill and will miss school you should (a) notify him that morning; (b) send your lesson plans to school for all periods during which you were to teach; and (c) notify your directing teacher as early as possible. Mr. Stevenson had told you that if you would ever be out, to be sure to notify him before he left for school, which is about 6:40 A.M.
Circumstances:	You awoke today at 6:30 A.M. with a badly upset stomach. You've been in and out of your bathroom for the last hour, and you've just decided that you won't be able to go to school today. You call Mr. Stevenson's home and there's no answer. You realize that he must already be in school so you call him there.
Simulation:	Mr. Stevenson comes to the phone and says, "Hello."

Reactions

1. What are you going to say? _____

_____

_____

_____

2. What will you do about your lesson plans for today's classes?

_____

_____

_____

_____

3. How could you have reduced the impact of your decision to

stay home for the day? _____

_____

_____

_____

_____

Effects   What effects will your actions and responses have upon Mr.
Stevenson? _____

_____

_____

_____

Your college supervisor? _____

_____

_____

_____

You? _____

_____

_____

_____

Notes   _____

_____

_____

_____

_____

_____

_____

_____

_____

_____

_____

_____

Caught in the Act

Setting:	Your classroom
Time:	During the lunch break
Person involved:	Miss Lee (your directing teacher)
Background information:	You have been a student teacher in Miss Lee's class for five weeks. You had some difficulties during the first few weeks, but everything is going better now. Your evaluation last week was the first really good one.
Circumstances:	Miss Lee was doing some writing at her desk while you were preparing for the next class. The school secretary just called your room and asked Miss Lee to come to the office. When Miss Lee left, you walked over to her desk to get a pair of scissors. On the desk was a personal letter Miss Lee had been writing.
Simulation:	You happen to see the letter and notice your name. So you pick up the letter and read, "Dear Maxine. We're into (your name)'s fifth week. Boy, this one still has a lot of growing to do. It's been a rough five weeks." Suddenly Miss Lee walks in and says, "What are you doing?"

Reactions   1. What will you say? _____

_____

_____

2. What is your opinion of Miss Lee's letter? _____

_____

_____

3. What error did you make? _____

_____

_____

4. What error did Miss Lee make? _____

_____

_____

_____

Effects   What effect will your actions and responses have upon Miss Lee?

_____

_____

_____

Your college supervisor? _____

_____

_____

_____

You? _____

_____

_____

_____

Notes   _____

_____

_____

_____

_____

_____

_____

_____

_____

_____

He Piles It On

Setting:	A college seminar room
Time:	During a student teacher meeting
Persons involved:	Dr. Melody (your college supervisor) and the other student teachers
Background information:	Dr. Melody has a reputation for having his students do a lot of work. He already has asked all of his student teachers to complete many forms, to develop an instructional materials list, and to turn in lesson plans for all teaching duties.
Circumstances:	You have been struggling to keep up with all of the obligations of student teaching. You have been very busy grading papers, planning lessons, and developing materials. Dr. Melody's work has made your schedule almost unbearable. Dr. Melody has just asked everyone to develop and type a resume within two days. You feel that assignment is unreasonable.
Simulation:	Dr. Melody looks right at you and says, "You look upset. What's wrong?"

Reactions

1. What are your objectives? _____

_____

_____

2. What will you say? _____

_____

_____

3. What do you expect your peers to say? _____

_____

_____

_____

Effects   What effect will your actions and responses have upon Dr.

Melody? _____

_____

_____

_____

Your peers? _____

_____

_____

_____

You? _____

_____

_____

_____

Notes _____

_____

_____

_____

_____

_____

_____

_____

_____

_____

_____

_____

For the Student Teacher

These simulations are a sampling of the kinds of unexpected events and problems that often face student teachers. Realize that they don't happen every day and that most of them can be avoided.

You need to be prepared to handle yourself in a professional manner. You should put a great deal of thought and energy into your student teaching responsibilities. With honesty, integrity, hard work, logic, and just a pinch of luck, you should have a successful student teaching experience. It is hoped that you will make your student teaching experience one that is devoid of the unexpected.

Chapter 9

Things to Remember

Being Prepared

Are you ready? Tomorrow—or soon after—you will be standing in front of your own group of students. As the teacher, you will have accepted the responsibility for the well-being and education of those students. You will also have accepted the fact that the handling of unexpected events involving parents, staff members, pupils, and others will be part of your duties. By having completed the exercises and simulations in this book, you certainly have gained ideas and experiences that will make you better prepared as you face unexpected occurrences.

Having an idea of what may happen will help you avoid some difficulties. And having rehearsed possible solutions to problems should make you realize that you are more ready to handle those that occur.

It certainly would not be wise for you to face each teaching day with great caution, as if fearing a catastrophe. However, just knowing about and having experienced the sample events in this book should help you realize that you are now better prepared.

General Guidelines

As you know, all of the simulations in this book are based on events that have actually occurred. Yet these events are only samples from an endless number of possibilities. It is logical to assume that the unexpected will continue. Here are six suggestions that should be very helpful to you as you face the unexpected.

1. *Know what is normal.* After you have gotten to know your students, their parents or guardians, the school personnel, and your school facility, you should often be able to predict the unexpected. Drastic changes in a student's attitude or appearance, unexplained building noises or

odors, strange comments, and your appraisals of persons could help you anticipate many difficult situations. Once you expect a problem, you can formulate and initiate a plan of action to reduce the event's impact or even to stop it.

2. *Stay calm and in charge.* When an emergency arises, others will look to you for guidance and direction. It is imperative that you appear calm, that you make decisions, and that you indicate to others what they should do. You, as the authority figure, will tend to establish the manner in which an unexpected event is perceived and handled.

3. *Don't be judgmental.* Remember that other persons have different standards, expectations, moral values, and so forth, based upon their own upbringing. You will need to consider these differences and realize that *your way* is not necessarily the *right way* for everyone.

4. *Assume you are being watched.* As you interact with others and make decisions, it is a good idea to assume that your principal, a group of parents, and a panel of your peers are all observing. That assumption will help you realize that every action you take may be closely scrutinized at some time. The assumption should also aid you in making appropriate decisions.

5. *Think about safety.* The wise teacher always considers the health and safety of his or her pupils. This teacher takes along another adult on field trips, keeps exit aisles and doors clear in case of fire, knows first aid, is aware of school emergency procedures, and so forth. Being continually aware of health and safety considerations will aid you in reducing the probability of a problem.

6. *Consider legal issues.* As you take actions and make responses to unexpected events, you should try to consider legal ramifications. If you act in a reasonable, logical, and appropriate manner, you should have no difficulty. Your principal should be an excellent resource regarding legal matters. He or she should be kept fully informed of all unexpected events and your actions so that you and the school can be properly safeguarded from a legal perspective.

Handicapped Students

Whether or not you are a special education teacher, you will undoubtedly have interactions with handicapped pupils. If you are in the special education field, you will regularly be teaching youngsters with handicaps. If you are in another area of teaching, you will no doubt have some responsibility for handicapped students. These youngsters may be mainstreamed into your classes. They may be in your homeroom. You may supervise handicapped pupils in the school cafeteria or during a study hall. Or you may simply be confronted with an unexpected event involving a handicapped pupil as you walk down the hall of your school.

In almost all ways, handicapped pupils are the same as others. They generally have the same needs, desires, and emotions as their nonhandicapped peers. Unless they are significantly retarded or disturbed, they probably will think and respond in ways similar to the norm.

You should try to interact with handicapped pupils in a very normal fashion. Speak in a regular manner with a blind student. Give clear directions. If the student doesn't understand or needs assistance, he or she will probably ask. Don't hesitate to use expressions such as, "It's nice to see you," or "See you later."

As you talk with a deaf student, be sure to speak normally and use appropriate gestures and expressions. Most deaf students are able to use some lip reading, so be sure to position yourself so that your face can be seen by the student. Writing a note is also appropriate. If you know some sign language, by all means use it.

A physically handicapped student usually only needs special facilities such as ramps or lowered work tables. Your regular curriculum and teaching procedures will generally be appropriate. Assistance may be needed by these students during an emergency evacuation.

Students who are retarded or emotionally disturbed may behave differently than others. When dealing with these pupils, you need to be very direct and clear with your instructions and statements. During an emergency be sure that these pupils know exactly what you expect them to do.

Health-impaired students may present certain risks of a medical nature. These medical problems should be known to the teachers directly involved. Teachers should be informed when these students are present so that appropriate reactions will be made in case of a sudden illness or accident.

Generally, students who are different need very little special assistance. Teachers should expect normal reactions and behaviors from these pupils. These students should not be "babied"; they should be treated just like everyone else.

Younger Students

When you work with very young pupils, you will face a variety of unexpected events. Most of the events can be handled in the way you rehearsed throughout this book.

The most critical aspect of this age group is one of communication difficulty. Very young children may not be able to explain how they feel or tell you what is wrong. With these children you will have to rely heavily on your observation skills.

Younger children usually don't have enough experience to understand the consequences of their behaviors. Thus, they may inadvertently cause accidents, become lost, or exhibit other illogical behaviors. Therefore, you must realize that close supervision is absolutely necessary.

Older Students

As children mature they change emotionally and physically. The changes associated with puberty and adolescence may cause problems related to emotional and physical maturation. Teachers who work with older pupils need to be ready to deal with such situations as teenage pregnancy, venereal disease, alcohol and drug use, and sexual behavior. Teachers may also expect to hear and be involved in students' dating and social problems.

Family and peer pressures regarding college, employment, and socializing may cause some particular problems within this age group. Achievement, physical ability, appearance, money, and competition may all be very critically related to adolescent behaviors.

If you are not judgmental and are able to listen well and dispense advice carefully, you will usually be of great assistance to your adolescent pupils. Remember, you may be the student's only adult friend, confidant, and counselor.

On Your Own

I hope you have answered yes to the question posed on the first page of this chapter, "Are you ready?" You have completed a variety of exercises designed to help you prepare for unexpected emergencies and difficulties. All the rehearsal in the world, however, cannot give you every answer you will need. The practice of handling unexpected events and the general guidelines presented, however, should make you ready to face the unexpected. Calm, logical reactions will enable you to make proper decisions so that the unexpected is of little consequence.

Remember, accidents and problems will occur. You will now be able to handle them well so that injury, damages, and consequences are minimal.

Enjoy your students. And enjoy being a teacher—a teacher who is now ready for anything.

Suggested Additional Readings

Chapter 2, Behavior Problems

Blanco, R. F. *Prescriptions for children with learning and adjustment problems.* Springfield, IL: Thomas, 1988.

Erickson, M. T. *Behavior disorders of children and adolescents.* Englewood Cliffs, NJ: Prentice Hall, 1987.

Gelfand, D. *Understanding child behavior disorders.* New York: Holt, 1988.

Molnar, A. *Changing problem disorders in schools.* San Francisco: Jossey-Bass, 1989.

Rutherford, R. B. *Bases of severe behavioral disorders in children and youth.* Boston: Little, Brown, 1988.

Chapter 3, Health and Safety

Derryberry, M. *Educating for health.* New York: NCHE Press, 1987.

Greene, W. H. *Introduction to health education.* New York: Macmillan, 1984.

Loya, R. *Health education.* Washington, D.C.: Library of Congress, 1983.

Smith, M. *Who teaches health?* Washington, D.C.: Department of Education, 1983.

Stern, B. *Society and medical progress.* Princeton: Princeton University Press, 1984.

Chapter 4, Students' Personal Problems

Altmaier, E. M. *Helping students manage stress.* San Francisco: Jossey-Bass, 1983.

Beane, J. *Self-concept, self esteem and the curriculum.* New York: Human Sciences Press, 1986.

Bonney, M. *Social psychology for school services.* New York: Human Sciences Press, 1986.

Levine, M. *Helping students.* Washington, D.C.: Department of Education, 1983.

Zins, J. E. *Helping students succeed in the regular classroom.* San Francisco: Jossey-Bass, 1988.

Chapter 5, Dealing with Parents

Gazda, G. *Human relations development.* Boston: Allyn and Bacon, 1984.

Levenstein, P. *Messages from home.* Columbus: Ohio State University, 1988.

Chapter 6, The Rest of the Staff

Clark, B. *Optimizing learning.* Columbus, OH: Merrill, 1986.

Classroom management. Springhouse, PA: Springhouse Corporation, 1987.

Kelly, J. *The successful elementary teacher.* Lanham, MD: University Press of America, 1985.

Mohr, M. M. *Working together.* Urbana, IL: National Council of Teachers of English, 1987.

Chapter 7, Your Personal Life

Cooper, H. *Pygmalion grows up.* New York: Longman, 1983.

Jones, R. *No substitute for madness.* Covelo, CA: Island Press, 1981.

Chapter 8, For the Student Teacher

Heywood, J. *Pitfalls and planning in student teaching.* New York: Nichols Publishers, 1982.

Mamchak, S. *The new psychology of classroom discipline and control.* New York: Parker Publication Co., 1981.

McIntyre, T. *The behavior management handbook.* Boston: Allyn and Bacon, 1989.

Posher, G. J. *Field Experiences: A guide to reflective teaching.* New York: Longman, 1985.

Roe, B. D. *Student teaching and field experiences handbook.* Columbus, OH: Merrill, 1984.

Rogers, D. *A handbook for students in the teaching profession.* New York: Thomas, 1987.

Chapter 9, Things to Remember

Handicapped Students

Anastasiow, N. *Development and disability.* Baltimore: P. H. Brookes, 1986.

Browder, D. *Assessment of individuals with severe handicaps.* Baltimore: P. H. Brookes, 1987.

Heward, W. *Exceptional children.* Columbus, OH: Merrill, 1988.

Musselwhite, C. *Adaptive play for special needs children.* San Diego, CA: College—Hill Press, 1986.

Reavis, C. A. *Extraordinary educators.* Bloomington, IN: Phi Delta Kappa Educational Foundation, 1988.

Sparks, D. *Managing teacher stress and burnout.* Lanham, MD: Aahperd, 1981.

Westwood, P. *Commonsense methods for children with special needs.* New York: C. Helm, 1987.

Zigmond, N. *Teaching learning disabled students at the secondary school level.* Reston, VA: Council for Exceptional Children, 1986.

Younger Students

Gearheart, B. *The exceptional student in the regular classroom.* Columbus, OH: Merrill, 1988.

Kindsvatter, R. *The dynamics of effective teaching.* New York: Longman, 1988.

Kourilsky, M. L. *Effective teaching.* Glenview, IL: Scott, Foresman, 1987.

Matson, J. L. *Enhancing children's social skills.* New York: Pergamon Press, 1988.

Strain, P. S. *Children's social behavior.* Orlando, FL: Academic Press, 1986.

Wolery, M. *Effective teaching principles.* Boston: Allyn and Bacon, 1988.

Older Students

Aggleton, P. *Rebels without a cause?* New York: Falmer Press, 1987.

Harris, P. *Evaluating and assessing for learning.* New York: Nichols, 1986.